Marco Polo

Marco Polo

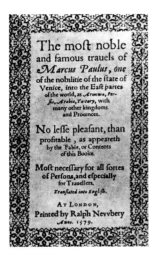

Jonathan Clements

HAUS PUBLISHING • LONDON

First published in Great Britain in 2007 by
Haus Publishing Limited
26 Cadogan Court
Draycott Avenue
London SW3 3BX

www.hauspublishing.co.uk

A CIP catalogue record for this book is available from the British Library

ISBN 978-1-905791-05-7

Typeset in Garamond 3 by MacGuru Ltd
info@macguru.org.uk

Printed in Dubai by Oriental Press

Cover pictures courtesy akg-Images

Contents

For Ian Everard

Introduction

Marco Polo (1254–1324) was born either in Venice, Italy, or Korčula in what is now Croatia. The son of a merchant family, he left Europe in 1271 on a trading mission with his father Niccolo and uncle Maffeo. The man who arrived back in Italy a generation later in 1295 was unrecognisable, but soon accepted as Marco by his relatives when he showed them the jewels he had brought back from the east. Captured in a later battle between rival merchant cities, he was briefly imprisoned, and worked on his memoirs with his cellmate Rustichello, an author of Arthurian romances who probably embellished the original text with some asides of his own. The result was *A Description of the World*, more misleadingly known as the *Travels*, which Marco appears to have planned as a merchant's guide to new markets, while Rustichello hoped to write a saga of marvels and martial valour.

This tension between these two collaborators has led to a confused view of Marco ever since. The original version of the manuscript has not survived – in fact, there may never have been a single text that we might reasonably call an 'original'. Instead, there were two or more variants, one favouring Rustichello's desire to amuse and entertain, another favouring Polo's business-like reports on potential foreign markets, still another containing opinions and revelations that the Polo family preferred not to be made public.

We can often see such disagreements in the text itself. Long,

Korčula in what is now Croatia, the possible birthplace of Marco Polo.

rather dreary lists of towns, often with very similar descriptions ('Three days to the west there is the town of X. The local people worship Mohammed'), are suddenly halted by agitated tangents, not of personal experience, but local legend and eastern folktales. If these are the interpolations of a frustrated co-author with aspirations to entertain, then we must sift through them in search of the real Marco, hunting down those few scattered moments in the text where Marco himself speaks: *I, Marco have seen this ... Messer Marco attests to this from personal experience ... so the local people told Marco when he was there.*

Marco Polo has always been a figure of some controversy.

The Toledo manuscript of his book, a Latin text often assumed to be the closest to the version not circulated in public, makes several allusions to practices that would have ruined his reputation in Christian Europe – references not only to casual sex, but also a liberal attitude towards non-Christian religions. Many of his public assertions were doubted in his own lifetime, by colleagues who refused to believe in such exotic marvels as coal or petroleum. In the centuries after his death, certain popular revels and plays in Venice may have included a stock character whose name was some variation on 'Marco Milioni' – a stuffy, millionaire Munchausen, always mumbling doubtful anecdotes and tall tales about his youthful travels. But many of Marco's supposedly bogus claims were made in his name by later authorities, who interpolated their own idle suppositions regarding such things as the history of ice cream or spaghetti. Illustrators of some later editions of his book added marvels of their own, associating him with outrageous stories that are not mentioned in the text. The most infamous scandal of all is the assertion that he never went to China at all, but made the whole thing up to while away his days in captivity.

Polo's fame rests largely on his book. His family was not particularly well off, his lineage not particularly noble. But his life spanned a remarkable moment in history, when, quite by chance, a Venetian merchant could enjoy trade privileges on the Black Sea, the friendship of a future Pope, and the sight of one of the last crusades. Marco Polo began his travels at the high point of the Mongol empire, just after an Islamic army had checked the Mongols' advance outside Nazareth, allowing him to visit the furthest corners of the known world, and to bring back stories beyond his readers' wildest dreams. He is known today as one of the few men before the modern age to walk between east and west, the confidant of an emperor and the guardian of a princess. Yet there is so much about Marco that we may never know, but instead can only glean from the gaps in his famous book: the things not said. As Marco would have us believe, half his fascinating story still remains untold.

Fraterna Compagnia

The route Marco followed was pioneered a generation earlier by other members of his family. The three Polo brothers, uncle Marco the Elder, Marco's father Niccolo, and uncle Maffeo, traded together as a *fraterna compagnia* – a family-centred partnership. As Venetians, the Polos enjoyed great opportunities in the 13th century Mediterranean.

At the beginning of the 13th century, Venetians had become involved in the Fourth Crusade, which began, at least in theory, as yet another military campaign to take back Jerusalem from its Muslim occupiers. The Venetians did not form part of the military contingent, but were largely involved as the owners of the ships that took the knights of Christendom to the Holy Land. However, shortage of funds led the Fourth Crusade in a new and controversial direction, not to the Holy Land, but first to Hungary, where the Crusaders attacked the town of Zara in order to obtain money to pay their Venetian shipmasters. It then took another detour to Constantinople, where it used its military might to overthrown the Byzantine emperor – a fellow Christian. While the Pope in Rome drafted stern rebukes to his soldiers, and ordered them to get on with their mission, the leaders of the Fourth Crusade tore Constantinople apart. The city itself was partitioned into quarters for the unexpected occupiers, and priceless Roman, Greek and Byzantine antiquities were shipped back to Europe.

Four bronze statues of chariot horses, said to have once decorated

The capture of Constantinople during the Fourth Crusade, from a Venetian painting.

Trajan's Column in Rome, were wrenched from their position at the Constantinople Hippodrome and taken back to Venice. Almost 50 years later, they were finally installed in their new home, close to the entrance to the Basilica of St. Mark (Basilica di San Marco), near the famous Piazza San Marco.

Marco Polo was born in the same year that the basilica got its new decorations. His father Niccolo was the middle brother of the three, working out of a house just north of the Piazza San Marco in the district of San Severo. At the time of Marco's birth, the main base of the company lay in the Venetian quarter of Constantinople, where, in the wake of the Crusaders, an entire sector of the city had been marked out exclusively for Venetian residents. The Polo family may have been closely involved with Constantinople for more than one generation – it is a strange coincidence that the two elder Polo brothers share the same names as the patron saints of Constantinople's Venetian quarter.[1]

Constantinople was not welcoming towards Venetians. The partitioning of the city and the continued rule of foreigners was a constant reminder of the atrocities of the Fourth Crusade. Marco's uncle Marco 'the Elder' maintained a permanent residence in Constantinople, but at some point in the 1250s, the family also began operating a trading post across the Black Sea, at Soldaia on the Crimean coast.[2] This marks the Polos out as a merchant family in search of a new niche. The big money, so it was thought, lay in the twice-yearly convoys from Constantinople, laden with many luxury items that had been popularised in Western Europe through the experiences of its crusader sons in the east. Exotic spices, oriental silks, ginger and cotton were bought at the borders of the Muslim world, sold at a mark-up in Constantinople, an even greater profit in Venice, and then distributed further to the West, by which point the price had become astronomical. It was not lost on the Polos that such price increases were a feature of every stage of the long trade routes from the east, and that the best profits were to be made by the trading company that could obtain the goods at the point furthest east and transport them west themselves, thereby cutting out as many middlemen as possible before reaching Venice.

The occupation of Constantinople and the partition of the old Byzantine Empire opened many new markets to Venetian traders. The Polos appear to have ignored the well-established and doubtless overpopulated trade routes from Venice to Alexandria and Acre, instead turning their attentions to the Black Sea coast. The Crimea was the termination of yet another trade route, north to the Baltic, where the Polos could buy furs, amber and honey from Russian traders. The trade was usually far less glamorous, bulk commodities such as salt, fish and corn, but it was in this latter item that the Polos struck it lucky.

Mongol warriors.

During the 1260s, poor harvests and famines caused the Venetians to rearrange some of their priorities. The market for luxuries dipped, while traders with ships full of grain found ready buyers. The three Polo brothers maximised their profits, using their positions in Soldaia, Constantinople and Venice itself to ensure that any 'middlemen' were members of their own organisation. The Soldaia establishment did well for them, but also encouraged them to consider even more distant markets.

The Mongol conquest of Central Asia brought death and destruction to those who did not immediately submit, and continued to concern many in Europe. Stories reached Western Europe of crushing defeats inflicted upon the Russians by Asian armies, the sub-tribe 'Tartar' often being favoured as a name for the whole, since it had a punning similarity to the Latin *Tartarus* – hell.

Nobody who had survived the sight of a Mongol army in action would have laughed off the threat. The Mongol mission was to conquer the entire world, and if left unchecked, they would surely arrive at the gates of Europe. However, there was even a degree of smug disinterest in some parts, when embassies arrived from some Muslim leaders, begging their former Christian enemies for help against a greater threat. In general, this was dismissed, with brush-offs such as the 'Let dog bite dog' of the Bishop of Winchester. However, the Mongols were regarded as a serious threat at the highest level. Pope Alexander IV issued *Clamat in Auribus* ('There rings in the ears ...'), a statement of his belief that Europe was under a terrible threat. But for the Polos, already trading in the edges of the Mongol Khanate of the Golden Horde, the rise of the Mongols was opening new opportunities.

It was, for example, now possible to trade directly with regions that had formerly been under Muslim authority, and even less welcoming to Venetians than Constantinople. With this in mind, the two younger Polo brothers joined a caravan that was heading north out of Soldaia, up the River Volga to Sarai.

Clamat in Auribus

'There rings in the ears of all ... a terrible trumpet of dire forewarning which, corroborated by the evidence of events, proclaims with so unmistakable a sound the wars of universal destruction wherewith the scourge of heaven's wrath in the hands of the inhuman Tartars, erupting as it were from the secret confines of Hell, oppresses and crushes the earth that it is no longer the task of Christian people to prick up their ears so as to receive surer tidings of these things, as though they were still in doubt, but their need is rather for admonition to take provident action against a peril impending and palpably approaching ...' – Pope Alexander IV, 1260[3]

The trade mission was experimental, an attempt to extend the Polo reach a little bit further into Asia, presumably with the hope of obtaining better goods, cheaper, and further increasing profits back home. Meeting with the local ruler Barka Khan (Berke), they traded with him in a manner that would have baffled many of their colleagues in Venice. The Polos paid 'tribute' to Barka by giving him jewels. As Marco recorded: *Barka took them willingly and was exceedingly pleased with them, and gave them goods of fully twice the value in return. These he allowed them to sell in many places, and they were sold very profitably.*[4]

Marco does not specify what the goods were, nor to whom the Polos were selling them. Some, presumably, may have made it back downriver to Soldaia, where their elder brother could ship them home. Others may have been traded with other Europeans – the Polos going through the elaborate façade of 'paying tribute' to Barka, but then selling off their 'gifts' in the more traditional manner to latecomers, or merchants who had not brought anything valued by the Khan.

Later European arrivals brought disturbing news. In 1261, while the brothers had been away from Constantinople, the city had been attacked by forces from Venice's enemy Genoa. The Genoese had successfully restored Michael VIII Paleologus, the rightful heir to the Byzantine Empire, overthrowing several decades of Venetian domination in the city. Reprisals in the Venetian quarter were swift, with some 50 merchants captured and mutilated by the victors. Many of them were blinded, a fate also shared by the 11-year-old boy who had supposedly been the ruler of Venetian Constantinople – blindness traditionally disqualifying a person from holding imperial power in the Byzantine empire. Michael VIII Paleologus embarked on a series of skirmishes in the Balkans to root out former allies of the Venetian usurpers. Although he would eventually sign treaties with Venice and restore some semblance of peace to the region, the Polos cannot have known that at the time. They would have rightly assumed that any Venetian in Byzantine territory could be in danger, and probably planned to avoid retracing their steps, hoping to head east around the edge of the Black Sea, to a Venetian enclave in Trebizond.

A medieval illustration of the Great Khan of China, with Marco Polo.

However, a second conflict made that impossible. At the beginning of 1262, Barka Khan went to war with his fellow Mongol Hulagu, ironically over similar religious issues to the ones that had started the Crusades. Barka, who had converted to Islam, was horrified at the part played by the Christian Hulagu in the destruction of Baghdad. The conflict represented the first signs of the disintegration of what had previously been a united Mongol Empire, as the grandsons of Genghis Khan began to lose touch with their steppe origins and develop local allegiances.

Although they were not directly affected by the war between

the two Mongol khans, the Polos were not prepared to risk travelling through the war zone. Instead, they headed east to avoid the fighting, settling in the city of Bukhara, in what is now Uzbekistan. There, they remained for three years, before a new opportunity arose.

An embassy arrived in Bukhara from Hulagu himself, on its way to seek audience with Hulagu's brother, Khubilai, the Great Khan. It seems unlikely that Hulagu's agents had undertaken the mission out of courtesy – he may have been hoping to enlist Khubilai's sympathies in the war with Barka, particularly since the ongoing spat had effectively shut down further Mongol conquests to the south and west.

Whatever the aims of Hulagu's embassy, he intended to impress Khubilai with gifts and stories from the far west. Marco himself recounted how his father and uncle suddenly acquired a new status as exotic curiosities: *And when the envoys beheld the two brothers, they were amazed, for they had never before seen Latins in that part of the world. And they said to the brothers: 'Gentlemen, if you will take our counsel, you will find*

Hulagu Khan 1217–65

A grandson of Genghis Khan, Hulagu was a full brother of Khubilai Khan. Both his mother and his wife were Nestorian Christians, an influence that led him to eagerly devote himself to the southward expansion of the Mongol empire at the expense of Muslims. In 1258 Hulagu's forces took Baghdad in the worst massacre in the Mongols' bloody history. With the death of the Great Khan Möngke in 1259, Hulagu returned home for the election of a successor. His Christian general Kitbuqa advanced on Muslim Egypt but was defeated at the battle of Ain Jalut. Hulagu's plans to avenge Ain Jalut were thwarted by his conflict with Barka. He was succeeded by his son Abaqa.

great honour and profit shall come ... the Great Khan has never seen any Latins, and he has a great desire to do so ... . If you will keep us company to his court, you may depend on it that he will be right glad to see you, and will treat you with honour ... whilst in our company you shall travel with perfect security, and need fear to be molested by nobody.'[5]

The entrance to the citadel of Bukhara.

Trapped for years in Bukhara, hearing only rumours of wars and persecutions back home, and faced with the opportunity to meet the Great Khan himself, the Polo brothers agreed.

When the brothers returned to Europe at the turn of the 1270s, they arrived as emissaries of Khubilai Khan himself, bearing letters for the Pope, requesting the dispatch of 100 learned Christians to Khubilai's court, ready to argue Christianity's case before him. Khubilai had also requested a vial of oil from the lamp that burned above the Holy Sepulchre in Jerusalem. The Polos arrived in Acre on the coast of the Holy Land and contacted the local papal legate Tedaldo Visconti, who informed them that the Pope had died. There would be no decisions made about further communications with the Mongols until a new Pope was chosen, a process which could take months, if not years.

On Visconti's advice, the Polos returned to Venice to await the election of a new Pope. *There Messer Niccolo learnt that his wife was dead, and there was left to him a son of fifteen, whose name was Marco. This was the Marco of whom this book speaks.*[6]

Berke Khan (d.1266)

The leader Marco Polo called Barka was the leader of the Golden Horde, the westernmost group of the Mongol Empire, charged with leading the Mongol attack into Europe. He served under his elder brother Batu in early successes against Poland and Hungary. However, Batu's khanate had gave up on invading Europe some time before, sulking after the selection of their cousin Ögedei as successor to the late Great Khan, Güyük. Although Berke occasionally raided into Poland after 1246, his campaigns were financially motivated, not part of a military campaign. His conversion to Islam in the 1250s set him on a collision course with his cousin Hulagu.

The Silk Road

As the months dragged on, still no new Pope was selected. Eventually, the Polo brothers gave up waiting. They wished to return to the east on another trading mission, and had no desire to wait so long that Khubilai died, made new contacts with other Europeans, or was cut off behind another war between his subordinates. The Polo brothers left Venice once more, taking the young Marco with them, and sailed for Acre in the Holy Land.

Despite the absence of a head of the church, wars in the Holy Land continued. The Polos arrived back in the Holy Land at the time of one of the last of the traditional Crusades. The Eighth Crusade, led by Louis IX of France, was intended to break the power of the Mameluke Sultans of Egypt. It left France in 1270 and headed not for the Holy Land, but for North Africa. However, the army was struck by disease soon after landing, and both Louis and his son died. The invaders were evacuated by Charles of Sicily, but a second fleet, sometimes called the 'Ninth Crusade', was already *en route* for Acre, under the leadership of Prince Edward of England (later Edward I).

Edward's sojourn in the Holy Land was notable for the company that he kept. He counted among his entourage a young Italian mercenary and entertainer by the name of Rustichello di Pisa, a would-be writer of Arthurian romances who may have met the young Marco at this time, and certainly met him many decades later.

An engraving of King Edward I of England (1239–1307), taken from a statue at Canarvon Castle.

While Edward's forces failed to gain any ground in the Holy Land, the Polos prevailed upon the papal legate Tedaldo Visconti. Although he was not even a priest, he was the most powerful papal official in the east, and was able to grant them permission to take the oil Khubilai had requested from the Holy Sepulchre in Jerusalem. More importantly, they also persuaded Tedaldo to write a letter to Khubilai, explaining the delays in the election of the Pope.

The Polos continued on their journey north along the coast to Layas, a port in the Cilicia area, not far from Antioch. Marco noted that it was: *a busy emporium. For you must know that all the spices and cloths from the interior are brought to this town ... and merchants of Venice and Genoa and everywhere else come here and buy them. And merchants and others who wish to penetrate the interior all make this town the starting-point of their journey.*[7]

Some variants of Marco's book report that they were delayed there by further fighting between Christian Mongols and Muslim Mongols, barring the route to the interior and making travel difficult. Other versions simply report that the Polo family were halted in Layas by a papal envoy, bearing the surprising news that a new Pope had been elected.

Tiring, like the Polos, of the seemingly interminable wait for a new Pope, local people in Viterbo had taken matters into their own hands, and barricaded the arguing cardinals inside their meeting hall. They ripped off the roof, exposing the cardinals to the elements, and allowed them only bread and water as provisions, until such time as they broke the deadlock over the

Pope Gregory X (c.1210–76)

Tedaldo Visconti was born in Italy, but spent much of his working life as Archdeacon of Liège. In this role, he had accompanied a mission to England, where he met Prince Edward, agreeing to accompany him on his mission to the Holy Land. As Pope, he remained devoted to the cause of regaining the Holy Land, and also tried, unsuccessfully, to broker a reunion of the Catholic and Eastern Orthodox churches, to repair the rift opened by the Fourth Crusade.

next Pope. The deadlock between pro-Italian and pro-French factions was swiftly broken; deprived of their luxuries, the cardinals took only three days to reach a compromise decision – the Polos' old friend Tedaldo Visconti. The news stopped the Polos in their tracks, causing them to hurry back to Acre for another meeting with him, shortly to be invested as Pope Gregory X.

Now invested with substantially greater authority, Tedaldo assigned them two Dominican friars, Nicholas of Vicenza and William of Tripoli, empowered to preach and ordain new priests in the east, and a new letter to Khubilai, encouraging him to support Hulagu Khan's Christian son Abaqa in a new Crusade against the Muslims. As a gesture of his friendship, he also handed the Polos many precious gifts for the Khan. The friars were nowhere near the requested 100 scholars, but they certainly represented the best that Tedaldo could provide at short notice and with limited resources. William, in particular, was one of Europe's leading experts on Islam, author of *Tractatus de Statu Saracenorum* (*A Report on the Condition of the Saracens*), which predicted that Muslim power was on the wane, that the Mongols would deliver the death blow to Islam's ailing fortunes, and that further 'crusades' in the east would require not military strength, but the application and diplomacy of missionary work.[8]

The Polos resumed their journey, but almost immediately lost their two travelling companions. Marco's book makes a garbled reference to the friars' fear of violence as they entered a war zone, falsely claiming that: *a great host of Saracens … ravaged the country, so that our envoys ran a great peril of being taken or slain. And when the preaching friars saw this they were greatly frightened, and said that go they never would … and took their leave, departing in company with the Master of the Temple.*[9]

The reference to the Master of the Temple seems strangely placed. The Grand Master of the Knights Templar at the supposed time of the Polos' journey was one Thomas Bérard, who died in battle in North Africa. But the reference here seems more likely to apply to his successor Guillaume de Beaujeu, who was in the Holy Land at the time, and called back to the west by Tedaldo in summer 1274 to organise what would have been another crusade, had Tedaldo not died during the planning stage.

If the friars really did depart with Beaujeu, then the Polos did not even leave the region until 1274, helping to explain one of the contradictions in Marco's book. His prologue glosses over the outward journey in short order, stating that: *Their journey back to the Khan occupied a good three years and a half, owing to the bad weather and severe cold that they encountered.*[10] However, the very same page states that, having ditched the friars, the Polos were able to reach the Khan after a winter and a summer. Reading between the lines, we might conclude that much of the alleged 'three years and a half' comprised the Polos' stops and starts in the Holy Land, and that they covered the bulk of the trip in a mere nine months.[11]

One of these false starts involved a journey to the south, towards the seaport of Hormuz, where the Polos hoped to take passage on a ship. It is widely believed that the organisation of Marco Polo's book loosely follows the tracks of his journey, particularly in the early stages as he headed out to China. But much of the text is concerned with stories, digressions and descriptions of cities merely in Marco's general vicinity. The text only rarely pinpoints Marco in particular places, but the first occasion in which it does places the travellers at Saveh, in Persia to the south of modern Tehran, where local legend held that the Magi, otherwise known as the Three Wise Men or the Three Kings of Orient, set out to take gifts to the newborn Jesus Christ.

In this city, wrote Marco, *they are buried, in three large and beautiful monuments, side by side ... Their bodies are still entire, with the hair and beard remaining ... Marco Polo asked a great many questions of the people of that city as to those Three Magi, but never one could he find that knew anything of the matter, except that these were three kings who were buried there in days of old.*[12] Marco found the confirmation he was looking for three days further on, at a town he called Kala Atashparastan, 'The Place of the Fire-Worshippers'. There, he claimed that local

Marco Polo at Hormuz, from the *Livre de Merveilles*.

people had confirmed the three kings were the Magi of Biblical legend, inadvertently causing trouble for his book in later generations, particularly among German critics who believed that the bodies of the Three Magi lay in Cologne cathedral, having been brought out of the east by the mother of the Emperor Constantine many centuries before Marco's birth.

The next personal appearance by Marco in the book that bears his name comes further to the south, near Hormuz, in the region of Rudbar. The area was often subject to raids by bandits Marco called the *Karaunas*, or 'mongrels', believing them to be the descendants of local women and Mongol invaders. Local superstition held that the Karaunas were able to cast a magical spell so that the day turned dark. *Marco himself narrowly evaded capture by these robbers in the darkness they had made. He escaped to a town called Kamasal; but many of his companions were taken captive and sold, and some put to death.*[13]

Could this have been the 'great havoc' that scared off the friars? It was certainly traumatic enough to cause a change in direction for the greatly reduced party. For some reason, even though the travellers reached Hormuz, they turned back, preferring instead to take an overland route. Marco's book praises the harbour of Hormuz, but comments that: *their ships are wretched affairs, and many of them are lost; for they have no iron fastenings and are only stitched together with twine.*[14] Marco also alluded to difficulties adjusting to the local diet, particularly the laxative qualities of date wine. His thoughts on Hormuz, perhaps reflecting his recent escape from bandit attack, seem obsessed with death and funerary rites. He twice mentions burial customs, possibly witness to the ceremonies for his otherwise unidentified travelling companions in the ill-fated caravan, and tells a story about the desiccated corpses of a band of attackers, seemingly defeated by the hot wind out of the desert.

After some years in the east in a state of relative fitness, Marco's luck ran out. For the next several pages of his book, ill health is a recurring concern, beginning with the date wine of Hormuz, and continuing

Relics of Alexander

Marco recounts that the kings of the Pamir region were descended from Alexander the Great (356–323 BC) and Stateira, the daughter of King Darius of Persia. The historical Alexander did marry a local girl, Roxana, but she left with him for the west, and did not return. Marco also notes a local legend that Alexander's steed Bucephalus sired a line of horses in the region, but it was extinguished when the breeder refused to let the local king, his nephew, have any of the horses. The breeder was executed, and his widow killed the remaining horses in revenge.

through a journey back to Kerman and up into the hills. The water of the Kerman trail, he writes, *is so bitter than no one could bear to drink it. Drink one drop and you void your bowels ten times over. It is the same with the salt that is made from it: if you eat one little granule, it produces violent diarrhoea.*[15] At no point does Marco explicitly state that he was troubled by such afflictions, but something certainly troubled him throughout his trek across Persia, only lifting as he and his fellow travellers climbed into the cooler, bracing air of the

Pamir mountains. *On the mountain tops the air is so pure and so salubrious, that if a man … falls sick of a fever … he has only to go up into the mountains, and a few days rest will banish the malady and restore him to health. Messer Marco vouches for this from his own experience.*[16]

Before long, the refreshing coolness of the mountain slopes became uncomfortable. *The region is so lofty and cold that you do not even see any birds flying. And I must notice also that because of the great cold, fire does not burn so brightly, nor give out so much heat as usual, nor does it cook food so effectually.*[17] Marco and his fellow travellers were approaching the edges of the world known to the Europeans, passing beyond the borders that had once been established by Alexander the Great, *through mountains all the time, climbing so high that this is said to be the highest place in the world.*[18]

Marco realised, perhaps in hindsight, that he was taking a path that Alexander had not. Whereas the armies of Alexander had descended to the south-east, towards what is now Pakistan, Marco's party continued to climb to the north-east, towards what is now the Uighur Autonomous Region of China, or Xinjiang. The Uighurs were a Central Asian people among the first to be conquered by the Mongols, and hence the first to be fully assimilated into the Mongol empire. Marco reported a land in which Muslims, Nestorian Christians and 'idolaters' (sometimes his term for traditional Chinese beliefs, sometimes Buddhism) mingled freely, even intermarrying.

'Marriage', or at least, some form of it, was a topic that interested Marco considerably in this region. Still relatively young and inexperienced, barely in his twenties, he reports three times on the relative sexual freedom of the area, particularly the willingness of women to enter into temporary marriage contracts. *If the husband of any woman go away upon a journey and remain away for more than 20 days*, wrote Marco in apparent guileless innocence, *as soon as that term is past the woman may marry another man, and the husband also may then marry whom he pleases.*[19] Marco's observations, first reported at the Muslim town of Pem, studiously avoid mentioning that he took advantage of such a custom, since doing so would have scandalised Christian Europe.

But reading between the lines of Marco's book, we find him undertaking the life-threatening crossing of the great deserts of central Asia, and finding what solace he can *en route*, particularly, it would seem, in the town of Kamul (Hami) to the north of the Gobi desert. The Toledo manuscript of Marco's book contains an extra passage not found in those distributed more publicly: *I give you my word that is a stranger comes to a house here to receive hospitality, he receives a very warm welcome. The host bids his wife do everything that the guest wishes. Then he leaves the house and ... the guest stays with his wife in the house and does what he will with her, lying with her in one bed just as if she were his own wife ... All the men of this province are thus cuckolded by their wives, but they are not the least ashamed of it. And the women are beautiful and vivacious and always ready to oblige.*[20]

Temporary Marriages

The concept of a limited-term marriage contract (in Arabic: *Nikahu'l Mut'ah*) is a feature of Muslim law in some areas, issuing from an interpretation of the Koran 4:24, which states that a secondary marriage is permissible if both parties agree a reasonable 'dowry'. Used in Shi'ite Islam (the Sunni sect does not recognise the loophole) for trial marriages, to overcome certain technicalities of cohabitation, and sometimes even to make it impossible for the participants to enter a full marriage with unwelcome third parties, it has other uses and abuses – most notably its application to a form of prostitution.

Such sexual dalliances sit in a chapter otherwise concerned with Marco's harrowing journey across the deserts of the region. He alludes to a week of 'refreshment' in the border town of Lop, before the arduous, month-long crossing of the Takla Makan desert, apparently often undertaken at night, to escape the worst heat of the day.

A truly arid place, devoid of vegetation and life and often

A giant Buddha statue from the Yungang caves in China, similar to those seen by Marco Polo.

conforming to the sand-dune stereotype of a desert, the 105,000 square miles of the Takla Makan was one of the most effective barriers between East and West. Marco's month-long crossing was the shortest possible route. Without a guide, travellers might inadvertently wander length-wise on a fatal journey lasting 600 miles, while even Marco's short route was attended by close calls with insanity and death. Marco wrote: *when travellers are on the move by night, and one of them chances to lag behind or fall asleep or the like ... he will hear spirits talking, and will suppose them to be his comrades. Sometimes the spirits will call him by name; and thus shall a traveller often be led astray so that he never finds his party. And in this way many have perished. Even in the daytime one hears those spirits talking. And sometimes you shall hear the sound of a variety of musical instruments, and still more commonly the sound of drums.*[21]

Marco rarely mentions any companions beyond his father and uncle, although he clearly travelled in the company of experienced desert voyagers. He notes that an associate of his, a Turk by the name of Zurficar, was once governor of the region for three years, but does not specify if he met him while travelling through, or in later years. Zurficar was in charge of the local asbestos-mining industry, which impressed Marco greatly, causing him to break of his text for a prolonged discussion of its magical properties, and his theory that the fire-resistant fibre was the origin of European legends about the impervious salamander, said to live in flames.

Having crossed the desert, the Polos now reached the towns of Su-chou (modern Dunhuang) and Kan-chou (Zhangye). Although he was still some way out of China proper, he had reached a point where many maps show the famous Great Wall to have its western terminus. However, Marco made no mention of the Great Wall, which, at this distant point and at the time of his arrival, would have been little more than a few isolated mud ruins, amid occasional misshapen and partly collapsed watchtowers.

Marco was far more interested in local religious customs, and may have visited the Big Buddha in Zhangye, which remains the largest reclining statue of Buddha in the world. Possibly unaware that he was witnessing the intermingling of both local Chinese and Buddhist traditions, he noted that the local 'idolaters' *have a vast quantity of idols; and I can assure you that some are as much as ten paces in length ... These huge idols are recumbent, and groups of lesser ones are set round about them and seem to be doing them humble obeisance.*[22]

But it was the behaviour of the Chinese that Marco was most taken with, particularly the popular habit of burning representations of worldly goods in order to confer them upon relatives in the afterlife. Marco was witness to a marriage ceremony between the spirits of two dead children. *They give the dead girl to a dead boy as a wife, and draw up a deed of matrimony. Then they burn this deed and declare that the smoke that rises into the air goes to their children in the other world ... They draw pictures on paper of men in the guise of slaves, and of horses, clothes, coins and furniture and then burn them; and they declare that all these become the possessions of their children in the next world.*[23]

In Xanadu

For the last 40 days of their trip to see Khubilai Khan, the Polos had a Mongol escort — quite possibly the entourage of the afore-mentioned Turk Zurficar, returning at the end of his own term of office. Marco, however, prefers to describe their fellow travellers as a personal escort sent by Khubilai himself, to welcome back the emissaries he had sent to the Pope so many years before.

After the muddled itinerary between their arrival in the Holy Land and their arrival in western China, they joined their Mongol escorts in the early summer of 1275, and headed north-west from Chagan-Nur (Mongolian: 'White Lake') to the city of Shang-du (Chinese: 'Upper Capital'), where Khubilai Khan could be found between June and August each year.

Shang-du began as a residence where Khubilai might escape the heat of a Beijing summer; the layout that Marco describes seems to reflect a Chinese capital in miniature. The central area was a walled hunting ground stretching for 16 square miles, *there are fountains and rivers and brooks, and beautiful meadows*, with a marble palace at one end. This constituted the 'inner city', like the Forbidden City in modern Beijing, an area exclusively reserved for the ruler of China. Clustered around its outskirts was the 'outer city', a place of civilian residence.

Khubilai had a second, temporary structure erected each year in a grove within the hunting grounds, constructed of large bamboo canes, *but with the interior all gilt and decorated with beasts and birds*

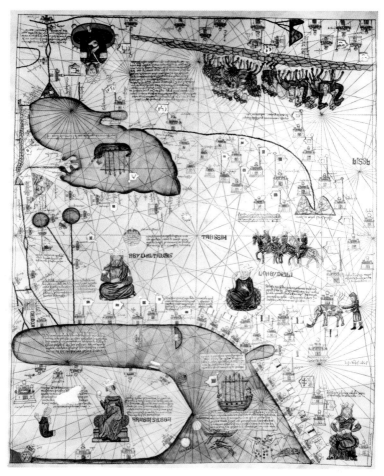

A panel from the Catalan World Atlas of 1375, showing the voyage of
Niccolo and Marco Polo.

*of very skilful workmanship. It is reared on gilt and varnished pillars,
on each of which stands a dragon, entwining the pillar with his tail and
supporting the roof on his outstretched limbs. The room is also made of
canes, so well varnished that it is quite waterproof.*[24]

At the time of the Polos' arrival, Khubilai Khan was 60 years old. Marco regarded Khubilai as the rightful heir to the overlordship of all the Mongols, although the historical records suggest that his seizure of the status of Great Khan came at the expense of his younger brother Arigböge, who had been proclaimed ruler in a rival council decision, and of his cousin Khaidu, who had been passed over in an earlier succession dispute. Khaidu was a representative of a faction among the descendants of Genghis Khan that did not want the Mongols to forget their roots. Already there were reports from the west of relatives converting to Christianity or Islam, 'going native' with catastrophic results, as in the case of the warring khans Hulagu and Berke. In a cunning compromise, Khaidu remained as the viceroy of the Mongolian heartland, where he and his supporters could assure themselves that they were maintaining the traditional Mongol way of life, while Khubilai busied himself with far more eclectic concerns to the south.

Raised in the full expectation that he would be put in charge of the conquest of China, Khubilai was already familiar with many aspects of Chinese culture. He had taken to heart the admonition of one of his Chinese advisers, that 'it is possible to conquer an empire on horseback, but not to rule it so' – a famous allusion to

Xanadu

Marco's description of Shang-du was to inspire the poet Samuel Taylor Coleridge (1772–1834) to compose one of his most famous works, the poem *Kubla Khan*, published in 1816 but written some time earlier. It begins:
'In Xanadu did Kubla Khan
A stately pleasure dome decree:
Where Alph the sacred river ran
Through caverns measureless to man
Down to a sunless sea.
So twice five miles of fertile ground
With walls and towers were girdled
  round:
And there were gardens bright with
  sinuous rills,
Where blossomed many an incense-
  bearing tree;
And here were forests ancient as the
  hills,
Enfolding sunny spots of greenery.'

the need for militaristic conquerors to learn more managerial roles in the aftermath of their victory.

Khubilai had a passionate interest in foreign cultures and ideas. Born of a Nestorian Christian mother, and attended by Chinese, Persians, Tibetans and Uighurs, he was ready to listen to any idea on its own merits. It is only here in the narrative, when Marco himself is present at Khubilai's court, that his book chooses to discuss in greater depth Khubilai's treatment of the elder Polos during their original visit, perhaps because it was only then that Marco saw how great the elder Polos' failing was. Khubilai's court was packed with foreign holy men and scholars – astrologers, diviners and philosophers. All contended for the Great Khan's attention with predictions, consultations and even what appear to have been conjuring tricks. Of all the old manuscripts of Marco's book, one alone, thought to be based on Marco's private notes, contains a prolonged speech by Khubilai, supposedly given to the elder Polos when Marco was still growing up in Venice.

'How would you have me to become a Christian?,' Marco has the Great Khan say, 'You see that the Christians of these parts are so ignorant that they achieve nothing and can achieve nothing, while you see that the Idolaters can do anything they please, insomuch that when I sit at the table the cups from the middle of the hall come to me full of wine or other liquor without being touched by anybody, and I drink them. They control storms, causing them to pass in whatever direction they please, and do many other marvels; whilst, as you know, their idols speak, and give them predictions on whatever subjects they choose. But if I were to turn to the faith of Christ and become a Christian, then my barons and others who are not converted would say: "What has moved you to be baptized and to take up the faith of Christ? What powers or miracles have you witnessed on His part?" … But now you shall go to your Pope and pray him on my part to send hither a hundred men skilled in your law, who shall be capable of rebuking the practices of the Idolaters to their faces, and of telling them that they too know how to do such things but will not, because they are done by the help *of the devil and other evil spirits, and shall so control the Idolaters that these shall have no power to perform such things in their presence. When we shall witness this, we will denounce the Idolaters and their religion, and then I will receive baptism; and when I have been baptized, then all my barons and chiefs will be baptized also, and their followers shall do the like, and thus in the end there will be more Christians here than exist in your part of the world.'*[25]

To a readership in Christian Europe, still smarting from the embarrassment of the loss of the Holy Land, with little hope of a new crusade, fearful of Mongol attacks by Muslim converts like Barka, Khubilai's words would have represented one of the most disastrous lost opportunities in history. No wonder the elder Polos had waited two whole years for the chance to speak with the Pope, if all he had to do was find the hundred smartest, most devout minds in his realm to challenge the holy men of other religions. A hundred of Europe's best scholars, and the wherewithal to transport them to Shang-du, would have been a colossal undertaking, but any expense would have been greatly outweighed by its potential benefits.

Nestorianism

In AD 431, Nestorius, the bishop of Constantinople, was thrown out of a church council for claiming that Jesus had been a human being. His banishment led to the formation of the 'Nestorian' off-shoot of Christianity, regarded by orthodox Christians as a heretical sect, but finding many converts in the east. Nestorian beliefs spread throughout Persia and Central Asia, as far as India, and even China, where a Nestorian inscription dating from AD 781 has been found. Several tribes of Mongols also converted to Christianity. Pockets of Nestorianism have survived to this day, but the bulk of its adherents were wiped out in the 14th century during the conquests of Tamerlane.

For a hundred years, there had been rumours in Europe of a mysterious Christian King of the East, a 'Prester John', who, it was hoped, might be found and persuaded to help fight the Muslims by attacking their rear as a new crusade invaded the Holy Land. These rumours, which reached the papal council in 1145, appear

An 18th-century image of Marco Polo.

to have originally been inspired by garbled accounts of a Mongol attack on the realm of the Seljuq sultan, conducted by a ruler whose army comprised large numbers of Nestorian Christians. Although actually a Buddhist, the leader Yelu Dashi somehow became corrupted into 'King John', whose grandson 'King David of India' was supposedly poised to attack the Muslim world from the east. A fake letter, purporting to be from Prester John, was received by Pope Alexander II, who sent emissaries with a reply to the east, although their fate is unknown.

For a mere moment, Khubilai had offered the Polos the chance to create Prester John for themselves, and to Christianise the East at a stroke. One can only imagine how pitiful the Polos' return trip must have seemed, starting out with only a pair of friars, and even then to lose them before they were out of the Middle East, finally arriving back at Khubilai's court some ten years later, almost empty-handed, but for some letters, a vial of oil, and Marco.

{They} paid their respects to him with all proper reverence ... Then they presented the credentials and letters which they had received from the Pope, wrote Marco, unaware that their friend Tedaldo was already coming to the end of his brief reign back in Europe. *{They} produced the oil from the sepulchre and at that, which {Khubilai} was very glad. And next, spying Marco, who was then a young gallant, he asked who was that in the company? 'Sire,' said his father, ''tis my son and your liegeman.'*[26]

Somehow, Marco entered the service of Khubilai Khan – it is implied that he was an unexpected hit due to his recollections of foreign countries, recounting anecdotes and observations that Khubilai's other ambassadors had failed to notice. As one of the few European visitors to the Mongol court, he was a valuable addition to Khubilai's group of advisers, at least until such time as he ran out of stories of European life. However, Marco was certainly not unique at Khubilai's court. He and his relatives were not even the first Italians to meet a Mongol khan, but there were many foreigners from other cultures who both preceded them and followed them. Chinese documents of the period do not draw distinctions between Europeans from one culture of another, or, say, between Europeans and Persians, but Marco would later allude to other white men in Khubilai's service.

Earlier Western visitors to Mongolia included John of Plano Carpini, an Umbrian missionary and former disciple of Saint Francis of Assisi, who unsuccessfully attempted to convert Khubilai's predecessor Güyük in 1246. Carpini is more famous today for a map of the world found bound into a copy of his *Tartar Relation*, thought for some time to include the first documented mention of 'Vinland' (Viking North America), until the map was found to be a fake. In 1249, the French missionary Andrew of Longjumeau followed in Carpini's footsteps, arriving at the time of the death of Güyük and failing to convert his successor. In 1254, the Flemish missionary William of Rubruck reached the court of Khubilai's brother Mongke, and returned to Europe with inspiring reports of the numbers of Nestorian Christians in the east. William's report was almost as extensive as Marco's, but less widely read, perhaps through his use of arcane Latin, or the lack of an amanuensis like Rustichello.

The China in which Marco arrived was not a single united entity. The region the Mongols had conquered included only northern portions – the Liao territories, Tufan and the realm of the Xi Xia, through which Marco and his companions had travelled from the west, and the territories of the later Jin dynasty, the former rulers of north China. Marco's writings recognised two Chinas. In the north, the area of the conquered Jin, was the region he called *Cathay*. The south, following the Mongol fashion, he called *Manzi*, the 'place of barbarians'. Although Marco's book called Khubilai the ruler of all China, this position was one he only gained in the years after Marco's arrival. At the time that the Polo family presented themselves at the Khan's court, battles were still raging in the south between Mongol forces and the last defenders of China's Song dynasty.

The Song Chinese were far from barbaric. Their dynasty had ruled China in some fashion for 300 years, but now only held the southern portion, ruling from a capital in what is now Hangzhou. It was Khubilai's intention to renew his assault on Song China in 1267, placing Marco in a fortunate position, as the witness to the final days of the Song.

In late August, when the weather to the south took a turn for the better, Khubilai's entourage prepared to leave Shang-du for the south. In what appears to have been a Mongol custom, Khubilai was expected to head south on 28 August every year in order to perform a ceremony rooted in his Mongol past. *The Khan keeps an immense staff of white horses and mares; in fact, more than 10,000 of them, and all pure white without a speck. The milk of these mares is drunk by himself and his family, and by none else, except by those of one great tribe that also have the privilege ... Now when these mares are passing across the country, and any one falls in with them, be he the greatest lord in the land, he must not presume to pass until the mares have gone by ... for they are to be treated with the greatest respect ... And ... the idolaters and Idol-priests ... say that it is an excellent thing to sprinkle {their} milk on the ground every 28th of August, so that the Earth and the Air and the False Gods shall have their share of it.*[27]

The Song Dynasty (AD 960–1279) The Song dynasty carved a new Chinese empire out of the chaos that followed the fall of the Tang dynasty in the early Middle Ages. Although the period is remembered as being one of China's cultural peaks, it was also one of great threats. The Song dynasty maintained an uneasy peace with non-Chinese peoples in the north, and lost the northern part of its realm to Jurchen invaders (the Jin dynasty) in 1127. The Jin formed an effective buffer between the Song and the Mongols, until the campaigns of Genghis Khan incorporated Jin territories within the Mongol empire in the early 13th century.

Although Marco explicitly refers to the ceremony as a custom involving the descendants of Genghis Khan, it may have been something else. Although Khubilai had not yet conquered south China, he pre-empted his own victory by proclaiming the foundation of a new Chinese dynasty in 1271. Even though the Song dynasty continued to hold out in the south, Khubilai had dubbed himself an emperor of the new Yuan dynasty, and retroactively elevated his ancestors to similarly imperial status.

While the custom Marco observes does seem tied to the steppe-nomad origins of the Mongols, it may have been a ceremony co-opted from the conquered Jin dynasty, one of dozens of Heaven-Earth rituals that a Chinese emperor was expected to perform each year, in order to ensure that he enjoyed the support of the gods.

With the ceremony complete, Khubilai's entourage began a month-long journey to the south, where it was his custom to spend each winter at the site of modern Beijing.

From the moment he meets Khubilai Khan until his arrival in Khubilai's winter capital, Marco's narrative is a veritable mess. It loses the geographically inspired symmetry of his journey east, instead drowning the reader in excitable paragraphs of reminiscences, observations and tangents. On occasion, Marco stops mid-flow to recount something he has previously forgotten, and his account of Khubilai the man, deprived of the place-by-place itinerary that has largely kept his narrative systematic, leaps around chronologically. He recounts, out of order, anecdotes separated by up to 20 years, overcome with enthusiasm for the sights and sounds of Khubilai's court.

At the time Marco wrote his book, either compiling his own notes or dictating to Rustichello, Khubilai was already dead. Marco thus had little to gain from a kindly portrayal of the Mongol ruler. The chances were negligible that Marco's text would have made it back to the Mongols, nor does Marco appear to have planned to return himself. His praise of Khubilai, and his portrayal of him as a stern but open-minded leader, hence seems devoid of anything

Khubilai Khan *circa* 1260.

but natural respect. Notably, however, his personal description of
Khubilai seems to date only from his earliest years in China. The
Khubilai that Marco met in the 1270s was *of a good stature, neither
tall nor short, but of a middle height. He has a becoming amount of flesh,
and is very shapely in all his limbs. His complexion is white and red, the
eyes black and fine, the nose well formed and well set.*[28] While this may
have been a fair description of the man Marco met on his arrival, it
does not tally with the portrait of Khubilai painted in 1280 by the
artist Liu Guandao, which shows a puffy-faced oriental potentate,

the most notable characteristic of whom is his extreme obesity. While Marco certainly may have met Khubilai, clearly had every admiration for him and may have spent many years in his loyal service, their time in each other's physical company may have only extended to a few weeks, or days, or even mere hours.

Khanbalikh

Marco Polo, and, presumably, his father and uncle, accompanied Khubilai as he headed south to his true capital. Khanbalikh (Turkish: 'the khan's city') was known to the Chinese as Dadu (Chinese: 'Great Capital'), although at the time Marco was there, the local accent probably made it sound more like *'Daidu'* or *'Taidu'*.

The city was located on the site of modern Beijing – in fact, Khubilai Khan was the first to establish it as the capital of all China. Under the preceding Jin dynasty, there had been a smaller city nearby that served as one of several administrative centres for the Jin. This Zhongdu (Chinese: 'Middle Capital') lay largely in ruins after the Mongol conquest, and was the subject of a local superstition at the time, faithfully reported by Marco. *{Khubilai} was informed by his astrologers that this city would prove rebellious, and raise great disorders against his imperial authority. So he caused the present city to be built close beside the old one, with only a river between them.*[29]

However, Marco's explanation seems to reflect the company he most often kept – the holy men and astrologers – rather than Khubilai's architects and planners, who had a simpler reason for building a new urban area. Zhongdu drew its water supply from a nearby spring that would not support a larger population, leading the planners of Khubilai's new, improved capital to build Khanbalikh as a completely separate walled capital just to the north-east, where residents could take advantage of two rivers and a series of lakes. Khubilai's personal palace was built just to the east of one of those lakes, and occupied the area of the famous Forbidden City of later emperors.

Despite this minor gaffe on Marco's part, the bulk of his description of the city that would later be known as Beijing is remarkably accurate. The city, wrote Marco, had *a compass of 24 miles, for each side of it has a length of 6 miles, and it is four-square. And it is all walled round with walls of earth which have a thickness of full ten paces at bottom, and a height of more than 10 paces; but they are not so thick at the top, for they diminish as they rise, so that at the top they are only about 3 paces thick. And they are provided throughout with loop-holed battlements, which are all whitewashed. There are 12 gates, and over each gate there is a great and handsome palace ... The streets are so straight and wide that you can see right along them from end to end and from one gate to the other ... All the plots of ground on which the houses of the city are built are four-square, and laid out with straight lines.*[30]

Marco goes on to describe suburbs beyond the main wall, where the foreign residents, including the Europeans, were quartered in different sectors, *as we might say, one for the Lombards, another for the Germans, another for the French*. This, however, appears to be merely a hypothetical example, since Chinese texts of the period do not distinguish between Europeans on any basis, categorising all of them as *Falang*, or 'Franks', and thereby suggesting that all the European visitors were quartered together, while other sectors served as suburbs for Persians, Indians, Japanese and similar ethnic groups.

It was in Marco's interest to imply that he was a rare figure in the east, but there may have been many more Europeans than he lets on. A generation earlier, in 1254, the Flemish visitor William of Rubruck reported many Europeans in Karakorum, the old capital of the Mongols before the conquest of China. Rubruck dined with a Parisian couple, the goldsmith Guillaume Boucher and his wife, who had been working in Belgrade when it fell to the Mongols, and been taken east as slaves, eventually finding work as jewellers and metalworkers to the Mongol court. They shared their captivity with, according to Rubruck, other Europeans, including a Greek physician who attended on the Khan, Russians, Frenchmen, and an Englishman called Basil. Even if the Mongols had brought no more slaves to the east in the decades since (which is unlikely), such people would surely have had children in Mongol service.[31]

The foreigners were a highly prized sector of the Mongol court, many of whom found employment as local administrators. The policy of Mongol conquest was to put foreigners in charge of newly conquered territory and in occupied north China, particularly Persians and Uighurs, who had had the opportunity to grow up under Mongol rule. Standing out very clearly among the conquered local Chinese, these foreign officials owed their lives and loyalty to the Mongols, and were less likely to develop local contacts with potential rebels. In recognition of their very different features, they were often referred to by the conquered Chinese as *semuren*, literally 'People with Coloured Eyes'. However, while Marco has much to say about the khan's entourage, the extent of the time he spent in Khubilai's direct company is debatable. Marco's descriptions of banqueting halls and the day-to-day running of Khubilai's palace imply that even during the summer recess, Khubilai's entourage numbered many thousands. It is possible that Marco engaged the Khan in direct conversation on his arrival, and did not get another chance until the following March. In the meantime,

'Sinful Women'

Moreover, adds Marco, no public woman {prostitute} resides inside the city, but all such abide outside in the suburbs. And it is wonderful what a vast number of these there are for the foreigners ... more than 20,000 of them. He goes on to reveal: *whenever ambassadors come to the Great Khan ... the captain is called upon to provide one of these women every night for the ambassador and one for each of his attendants.* However, Marco neglects to suggest that he must know this because he was one such 'ambassador' himself.[32]

however, he was present as an observer in a scandal that shook Khubilai's court.

One of the *semuren* was Ahmad Fanakati, a Muslim from Tashkent who had served the Mongols in the north for 22 years, before being savagely murdered.[33] The surprising twists of fortune of the investigation into Ahmad's demise were to give Marco a unique appreciation of both Mongol administration and Mongol justice at work.

Ahmad enjoyed such a high position of trust with Khubilai that he had effectively become the viceroy of much of north China. *This person disposed of all governments and offices, and passed sentence on all malefactors*, wrote Marco, *and whenever he desired to have anyone whom he hated put to death, whether with justice or without it, he would go to the Emperor and say: 'Such a one deserves death, for he has done this or that against your imperial dignity'. Then the Lord {Khubilai} would say 'Do as you think right,' and so he would have the man forthwith executed.*[34]

However, Ahmad's long period in office was brought to an abrupt end when a group of Chinese conspirators, posing as visiting Mongol dignitaries, dazzled him with torchlight and beheaded him before he could see their true faces. Ahmad's own entourage retaliated immediately – his murderer was killed by an arrow where he stood, although other conspirators went to ground, and were only rooted out after a series of investigations by Ahmad's lieutenant Kogatai.

And you should know, notes Marco, *that all the {Chinese} detested the Great Khan's rule because he set over them governors who were Tartars, or still more frequently Saracens, and these they could not endure, for they were treated by them just like slaves.*[35] Rebellious feeling ran to such heights, it seemed, that the murder of Ahmad was merely one small element in a nationwide uprising against 'everyone with a beard' (i.e. all non-Chinese men), although the Mongol clampdown seems to have nipped it in the bud. Marco, and his readers, had every reason to be impressed, not only by the Mongols' hold on power, but in the subsequent enquiries.

When Marco arrived in Khanbalikh, he witnessed Khubilai's full investigation, in which the tables were soon turned on the alleged victim Ahmad. Far from uncovering a conspiracy, Khubilai's investigators determined that Ahmad's murderer had himself been avenging an injustice. Only now did it become apparent that Ahmad's murderer had a mother, daughter and wife who had all been raped by Ahmad under various pretexts.[36] That, at least, was how Marco understood the final ruling, which saw the body of Ahmad exhumed and thrown to the dogs, his supposedly ill-gotten gains transferred to Khubilai's treasury, and seven of his sons executed.

Whether this was Mongol justice at work or the conspicuous use of a scapegoat to appease local complaints among Mongol subjects, the downfall of Ahmad initiated a decline in Khubilai's respect for the Muslim religion. *These circumstances called the Khan's attentions to the accursed doctrines of the Saracens, which excuse every crime, and even murder itself when committed {against those} who are not of their religion. And seeing that this doctrine had led the accursed Ahmad and his sons to act as they did without any sense of guilt, the Khan was led to … the greatest disgust and abomination for it. So he summoned the Saracens and prohibited their doing many things which their religion enjoined.*[37]

Khubilai's anger at the Muslims is one of the rare places where Marco's book states outright its narrator's attendance – *And at the time when all this happened, Messer Marco was in this place.* But Marco's account of events misinterprets certain elements – at least in the version that survives in modern times, mixing several separate incidents at Khubilai's court. Possibly Rustichello, in search of a human face to put to a story of religious issues, preferred to make it sound as if Ahmad was responsible for all the anti-Muslim feeling in the period.

The same events are described in more logical order in the *History of the Mongols*, a later 14th-century Persian account by the Muslim convert Rashid al-Din. Rashid adds tantalising extra details, such as the fact that Ahmad's killer was not only a Chinese turncoat, but a fellow official who had already made one previous attempt on his life, only to be pardoned by Khubilai for later help securing the surrender of the city of Xiangyang. Despite their enmity, the two men were obliged to work together for nine years of what must have been intensely unpleasant office politics, before their rivalry broke out again into open conflict. Rashid describes events in a similar fashion to Marco, and adds that Ahmad's posthumous fall from grace was largely caused by the discovery of his widow wearing jewels that Ahmad had been supposed to pass on to Khubilai.[38]

Marco claims that Khubilai punished all Muslims for Ahmad's misdeeds, demanding that they take their wives *according to the law of the Tartars*, and seemingly also forbade them from slaughtering animals in *halal* fashion. But Rashid reports different origins for the flurry of anti-Muslim feeling in China; while Ahmad's corrupt behaviour certainly may not have helped, it was two other incidents that caused real difficulty for local Muslims.

The first involved a group of visiting Muslim dignitaries from the vicinity of Lake Baikal, who offended Khubilai by refusing the offer of dishes from the Khan's own table at a banquet, explaining that his food was not *halal*. Reared on the harsh protocols of Mongol hospitality, and perhaps also imbued with a Chinese sense of losing face, Khubilai was deeply embarrassed by such a refusal from his own guests, and angrily ordered that all people, regardless of their religion, should henceforth slaughter their animals in the Mongol fashion.

Rashid claims, and there is no reason to doubt him, that enemies of the Muslims within the court saw this as their chance to gain extra ground. Realising that devout Muslims would be reduced to slaughtering their own *halal* livestock in secret, they offered a reward to any slave who would inform on his master. Before long, reports both true and false began to arrive from servants, saying that Muslims all across the city were directly disobeying the Khan's order in their own homes.[39]

This alone was enough to lead to purges, banishments and executions in Khanbalikh, and the number of Muslim merchants visiting China began to fall noticeably. But it was a second argument, alluded to by both Rashid and Marco, that was the last straw for Khubilai. The same troublemakers brought the ninth chapter of the Koran to his attention, particularly two passages in it that appeared to call for the deaths of those who worship more than one god.

Khubilai called for the leading imam in Khanbalikh, demanding to know if the phrase really existed, and if it did, why the Muslims had not yet carried out their supposed duty to commit genocide.

'The time has not yet come,' was the chilling reply, 'and we have not the means.'

'I at least have the means!' said the irate Khubilai, and ordered the execution of the imam.

This, it seems, is a prime candidate for Marco's 'accursed doctrine of the Saracens', and we should perhaps not be too surprised that Marco leaves the story early, instead of supplying the ending to be found in Rashid. Presumably with the entire Muslim population of China facing imminent massacre, Khubilai's Muslim courtiers pleaded with him to seek a second opinion before taking one imam's word as the policy of all Islam.

One Hamid al-Din from Samarkand realised the reason for the Khan's sudden panic. As one who tolerated all religions at his court, Khubilai risked being regarded as a 'polytheist', and, depending on how one translated Koran 9:5 and 9:36, the passages might be seen as calling for the Khan's own death. Instead, Hamid explained: 'Such a one is a polytheist who does not recognize God,

From the *Livre des Merveilles*, a representation of the Khan's palace at Khanbalikh.

and attributes companions to Him, and rejects the great God.'[40]

In other words, since he did not reject the One God, Khubilai was safe. While the public version of Marco's book gleefully reported the repudiation of Muslim customs, in private he acknowledged that Khubilai still maintained an even-handed approach towards the faiths that jostled for his attention.

Marco's private notes, uncirculated in most editions of the book, record that 'all the Christians' in Khubilai's company were summoned for an Easter celebration in the Khan's company. At first, this might seem like exactly the sort of thing Marco would want in the public version of his book, but he must have known that Christian European readers would not have taken kindly towards the Khan's attitude to rival faiths.

Learning that this was one of our chief festivals {Khubilai Khan} summoned all the Christians, and bade them bring with them the ... Four Gospels. This he caused to be incensed many times with great ceremony, kissing it himself most devoutly, and desiring all the barons and lords who were present to do the same. And he always acts in this fashion at the chief Christian festivals such as Easter and Christmas, {and} at the chief feasts of the Saracens, Jews and Idolaters. On being asked why, he said: 'There are four prophets worshipped and revered by all the world.

The Christians say their god is Jesus Christ; the Saracens, Mohammed; the Jews, Moses; the Idolaters, Sogomon Borcan [Shakyamuni Buddha], *who was the first god among the idols; and I worship and pay respect to all four, and pray that he among them who is greatest in heaven in very truth may aid me.'*[41]

Khubilai's attitude may have been a genuine syncretism and respect for all religions, or a means of hedging his bets. There is certainly an element of prevarication in his refusal to carry a crucifix before his army – he told Christian members of his entourage that it was out of

The Khazars

The presentation of Khubilai in Marco's text bears a close resemblance to the story of the Khazars, a Turkic community in the north Caucasus, on the shores of the Caspian Sea, who legendarily converted to Judaism *en masse* after weighing up the evidence from competing missionaries. They were conquered by the Rus in the 10th century, but their religious example would have been very tempting to missionaries from other faiths, hoping to repeat a similar mass conversion among the Mongols.

respect for Christ, although it is more likely that he wished to avoid irritating his non-Christian followers. While the Mongols enjoyed a reputation as savage conquerors, Khubilai appears to have hoped to manage the various races under his control as harmoniously as possible.

Such tensions within Khubilai's entourage bring a crucial factor to the fore. Marco is renowned throughout Europe for his travels to China, but for all the time that he was there, he was a guest in an occupied country. The China that Marco saw had elements of the traditional culture, but was also a conquered territory under stern administration by a foreign power. Marco's experience of China was not the immersion of the anthropologist or emigrant, but the misunderstandings of a foreign tourist or diplomat. He never learned Chinese, and seems to have largely associated with non-Chinese people – his fellow, unnamed Europeans, Muslim *semuren* or Mongol officials. With so many Central Asian officials among its staff, the Mongol administration often used Persian as a *lingua franca* – causing much of Marco's discussion of Chinese places and peoples to be filtered through a foreign language.

As a European traveller, able to boast of personal acquaintance with the current Pope, conversant in the trade languages of the Middle East after several years in the Holy Land and points east, Marco had quite accidentally chosen the perfect time to travel. The Mongol conquest had opened up a relatively safe road between Europe and the Orient, but it had also opened up countless opportunities towards the south-east, as Khubilai's armies conquered China.

Far to the south, Khubilai's armies were crushing the last defenders of China's Song dynasty. The last Song emperor of any ability, Duzong, had died suddenly in 1274, leaving three sons, from whom the four-year-old Gongdi (r.1274–8) was selected as his successor. His mother and grandmother acted as regents, and it is one or both of these women to which Marco refers when he writes of the 'queen of the realm' of south China.[42]

While Song loyalists clung to the southern city of Hangzhou, Gongdi's surviving relatives were evacuated even further to the south. The Mongol general Bayan enjoyed a swift southward advance, before which most Chinese cities simply surrendered to avoid further conflict. The regents, however, were intent on preserving their dynasty, and wrote to Bayan with an offer to acknowledge the Mongol rulership of the north, and when this was refused, a further offer to pay annual tribute to Khubilai Khan, if he would only leave south China intact and unthreatened. Apparently, this letter was written in Mongol or Persian, since Marco claimed to have read it himself some years later.

General Bayan, however, refused to accept anything but unconditional surrender, leading both the regents and the emperor to hand themselves over to Mongol forces. To many minds, this was the end of the Song dynasty, although the child-emperor's elder brother continued to be the figurehead of a resistance movement even further to the south. The younger 'queen' and the deposed Song emperor were brought to Dadu, where Khubilai acknowledged their surrender and installed them in palatial residences. According to Mongol accounts, the defeated Chinese were treated with great sensitivity – largely to preserve the image of the Mongols as caring administrators, the former emperor was created a duke in the new regime. Life in Dadu, however, does not seem to have been as trouble-free as the conquerors wished. Two serving maids of Gongdi's mother hanged themselves in protest at an unrecorded insult, causing Khubilai to angrily order that their corpses be exposed (quite possibly the same punishment of 'leaving them for the dogs' as was meted out to Ahmad), while the heads were hung in the former regent's chambers and left to rot in full view.

This severe punishment led to an argument between Khubilai and his wife Chabi, in which her requests for the surrendered nobles to return to their true home in the south were refused. Chabi was put in charge of the care of the defeated nobles, and attempted to make their stay at the Mongol court more comfortable.

Notably, the story of the capture, suicide, retribution and reconciliation is precisely the kind of gossip and scandal that would have thrilled Marco, but is not mentioned anywhere in his book.[43] Either Khubilai's entourage swiftly covered up the events for the sake of public relations, or Marco was simply not as close to palace events as he had previously implied. The best he can do, instead, is simply to mention that the 'queen' of the south *was conducted to the Great Khan. And he, when he saw her, directed that she should be treated with honour and consideration as befitted a great lady.*[44] This is not necessarily evidence that Marco was not in Dadu at the time, but it strongly suggests that by the time of the scandal of the suicidal maids, Marco was already away from the capital, and heading south on one of several missions for Khubilai. He was no longer a visitor in the Khan's court, but one of the *semuren* administrators, serving the new regime as an official.

The Fork in the Road

Through comparisons of Marco's observations with events confirmed by other writers and histories, we can determine that Marco undertook two or perhaps three journeys to the south-west in the course of his sojourn in China. At least one of them occurred before 1280, and may have even occupied him in the period 1276–7.[45]

Marco's account does not specify why he went to the south-west, through mountains of China and Tibet, and onward into north Burma, although his claim of 'business for the Khan' tallies with a military expedition undertaken on Khubilai's borders in the same period. The main thrust of the Mongol invasion swept to the south-east, fighting the last defenders of the Song dynasty. Marco, however, appears to have headed to the south-west, possibly in the wake of the Uighur general Arigh Khaya, whom Chinese sources record as leading an army of 30,000 soldiers towards Burma.

While Marco followed the roads to the south-west, the defenders of the Song ruler made their last stand. Emperor Duanzong (r. 1276–8) was only eight years old when he was hastily crowned as a successor to his younger half-brother Gongdi. Retreating first to the sea port of Fuzhou and then coastal towns further south, he nearly drowned during one evacuation, and never quite recovered. After his death, his younger brother supposedly took over, but his 'supporters' realised that all was lost at their defeat in the naval battle of Yamen, off the Canton coast. His ship sinking, minister-

The Marco Polo Bridge.

in-exile Lu Xiufu grabbed the last boy-emperor and jumped into the sea. Scattered remnants fled to what is now Vietnam and Thailand, but never mounted an effective resistance. All China was under Mongol rule by the end of 1279.

Ten miles out of Khanbalikh, Marco reached a place that would, quite by accident, become one his best known discoveries – a stone bridge spanning a river. The description has become a little garbled in transmission, with Marco's text apparently calling the river Pulisanghin, although the term is actually Persian for 'stone bridge'. *It has very few equals*, wrote Marco. *The fashion is this: It is 300 paces in length and it must have a good eight paces in width, for ten mounted men can ride across it abreast. It has 24 arches and many water mills, and is all of a very fine marble, well built and firmly founded. Along the top of the bridge there is on either side a parapet of marble slabs and columns made in this way: At the beginning of the bridge there is a marble column, and under it a marble lion so that the column stands upon the lions loins while on top of the column there is a second lion both being of great size and beautiful sculpture. At the distance of a pace from this column, there is another precisely the same, also with its two lions and the space between them is closed with slabs of grey marble to prevent people from falling over into the water. And this the columns run from space to space along either side of the bridge, so that altogether it is a beautiful object.*[46]

It may seem like a remarkably minor, and possibly rather dull passage in Marco's narrative to single out for worldwide fame. What Marco cannot have known at the time he wrote was that the bridge would somehow survive the centuries that followed. It still stands today, a few miles outside modern Beijing, its flagstones worn into gentle curves, its many lions still standing atop their protective pillars. Not all the lions date back to Marco's time – many have been replaced in later dynasties, and the bridge itself was substantially restored during the Qing dynasty, but some lions are demonstrably as old as Marco Polo, and some even older. Its Chinese name is *Lugou*

The Marco Polo Bridge Incident

The bridge is not famous merely because Marco described it. Its worldwide notoriety only truly arrived on 7 July 1937, when it became the flashpoint of conflict between the invading Japanese and local Chinese Kuomintang troops. The gunfight at the Marco Polo Bridge marked the opening shots of the Second Sino-Japanese War (1937–45), itself the opening phase of the Second World War.

Qiao ('Bridge on the Cottage/Black/Lu Family Waterway') but it is known in most European languages as the Marco Polo Bridge, after the man who first described it to a European audience.

Marco's description of the bridge that now bears his name is cited as one of the proofs of his genuine presence in China, although the historian is forced to forgive a few slips – his misidentification of the bridge's actual name, and the fact that the modern bridge lacks the same count of arches Marco describes. It is, however, a firmly identified geographical location, which has been used as part of the many arguments over the veracity of Marco's text. Once over the bridge, Marco himself wrote that the road forked in two directions, *one branch going westward through Cathay, the other south-*

eastward towards the great province of Manzi.[47] In other words, even as he embarked upon one of his great journeys within China, he was turning away from much of what European readers would come to regard as 'Chinese', heading back towards the west.

Some of Marco's critics have commented that he has surprisingly little to say about famous elements of Chinese culture. There is, for example, no talk in Marco's book of the Great Wall, nor of tea or footbinding. Setting aside the possibility that he simply had not yet got round to bringing them up, a point he legendarily raised himself on his deathbed, the typically 'Chinese' omissions were far less likely to come to Marco's notice while he was in the service of an occupying power.

The Great Wall of China, as we know it today, is an impressive construction, but its modern spectacle only dates back to the days of the Ming dynasty. At the time of Marco's arrival in China, the 'Great Wall' was not a massive stone fortification, but a series of dilapidated walls of rammed earth, allowed to slide into neglect by successive dynasties, and ignored by the Mongols, whose territory encompassed it on both sides. Even if Marco had passed a section of the Great Wall on his way into China, there is a good chance he might not have even noticed it – he would have had to be looking up from his horse or out from his carriage at the right moment, or have it pointed out to him by someone who actually cared. Even today, much of the grandeur of the Great Wall is difficult to appreciate from ground level. The knowledge that it stretches for thousands of miles out of direct sight can often be more impressive than the sight itself.

Similar possibilities help explain Marco's lack of interest in other 'Chinese' customs. Marco did not live in China as a farmer or herdsman – he was placed high up in the social order, in what we today might call the 'middle class', as part of an administrative elite with little interest in the day-to-day life of the people who had been conquered. He has much to say about Chinese liquor, demonstrating a medieval European interest in wine as a drink with less chance of contamination than water. Tea crops could have been disrupted in the upheavals of the Mongol conquest, and although the boiling of the water would have rendered it safe for consumption, such hygienic concerns would not necessarily have come to Marco's attention. He may simply not have been interested.

As a speaker, and, we presume, reader of Persian and Mongol, Marco had little use or interest for the complicated writing system of the conquered Chinese population. Nor did he have much interest in the strange customs of their inner chambers – Marco has much to say about the womenfolk of China, particularly in the less widely circulated Toledo manuscript, but his observations are mostly concerned with ethnic populations whose women never practised footbinding, or the Mongols themselves, who were similarly uninterested in hobbling their womenfolk. Although a popular development in the preceding Song dynasty, footbinding itself may have fallen out of fashion in the generation that Marco spent in China. It was formerly a prerogative of the idle Chinese rich, but with wealth now concentrated in the hands of Mongols and pro-Mongol collaborators, how many Chinese would take the risk of crippling their daughters for the sake of a fashion that was no longer that of the ruling elite?

Footbinding

Beginning late in the Tang dynasty (AD 618–907), footbinding was a strange custom among the Chinese elite. The feet of girls were tightly wrapped in infancy, and kept under constant pressure, crushing and breaking the smaller toes, and creating a pus-ridden, hoof-like stump by the end of childhood, rendering the victim unable to walk without intense pain. Such 'lotus hooks' or 'lily feet' were considered highly desirable by the Chinese upper classes. However, they were regarded as vulgar and barbaric by many ethnic minorities, including the Mongols. The possibility remains that footbinding in Marco's time was far less severe than in the much later Qing dynasty (AD 1644–1912), from which our only photographic evidence comes.

Perhaps more tellingly, although footbinding is a well-known feature of medieval Chinese life, actual sight of bound feet was taboo at the time. Seeing a bound foot up close would have required an intimacy unavailable to any man but a woman's husband. It seems churlish to criticise Marco for not knowing of a custom that was out of favour and deeply private, particularly when he spent so much time away from the place where it was common.

Although Marco believed himself to be in 'China', his definition, our definition, and the definition of the contemporary Chinese are all slightly at odds. He had arrived in a north China under Mongol domination, itself seized from non-Chinese usurpers before his arrival. He then headed south-west, briefly through 'real' Chinese territory, before the fork in the road past the famous bridge took him away from the main population once more. The extent of his mission thereafter kept him largely within the borders of the modern People's Republic of China, but in south-western regions dominated by ethnic groups such as the Tibetans, the Bai, the Mian and the Hui. Saying that Marco was still 'in China' is a statement loaded with political associations. Our own concept of Chinese race is largely concerned with the attitudes, customs and history of the Han ethnic group, which dominates modern China but is in short supply in its south-west. On this trip, Marco was dealing with people whom modern Chinese politicians would not hesitate to call Chinese, although their clothing, native language and customs might have often been at odds with Han Chinese behaviour.

During Marco's journey to the south, he picked up several local legends which somehow became entangled in his mind with the story of the mythical eastern Christian king 'Prester John' – Marco does not seem to have accorded much credence to the Prester John legends, since he had already worked out for himself that the closest possible real-world analogy would be Nestorian Christianity and the possible future conversion of Khubilai himself. The

Chinese stories dated from wildly different historical periods, but it seems that to Marco's European ear, the difference between the nation of Jin (706–403 BC), the dynasty of the Jin (AD 1115–1234) and the dynasty of Qin (221–206 BC) would have sounded close enough as to make no odds. Nor can it have helped that the *Jin* of 'Jin dynasty' also means 'gold' in Chinese – factors that formed a heady cocktail of legend, and became Marco's tale of the 'Golden King'.

Marco believed that a Golden King had built the castle of Xiezhou, an old fort remodelled and expanded a generation before Marco's arrival. A vassal of Prester John himself, or so Marco thought, the Golden King rebelled, but was brought down by seven agents of Prester John, who joined his entourage as loyal subjects, worked their way up through the ranks, and then kidnapped him. Dragged before Prester John and begging for mercy, the Golden King was permitted to live as a cowherd for two years, before being restored to his former life, his lesson presumably learned.

In recounting the story, Marco appears to mix several Chinese tales, notably that of Baili Xi, a minister of an ancient Chinese state, forced to become a refugee after his king refused to listen to his advice, leaving his country open to assault by the ancient state of Jin. Forced to work as a cow-herd in a neighbouring kingdom, Baili Xi was eventually recruited by agents of the state of Qin, yet another kingdom, but one with a reputation for hiring officials on the basis of their ability, not their ethnic origin.[48]

Once again, in-depth discussion of sexual customs can only be founding Marco's more private 'Toledo manuscript', outlining what he believes to be curious local practises, although much of what he describes could be the imposition of sexual conquest by the new masters of the Tibetans. *Some residents*, he writes, *have beautiful wives and offer them to passing traders. And the traders give the women a … trinket of some trifling value. Having taken his pleasure for a*

A garden house on a lake in Yunnan.

while, the trader mounts his horse and rides away. Then the husband and wife will call after him in mockery: 'Hi, you there – you that are riding off! Show us what you are taking with you that is ours!'[49]

Once across the Yellow River, *too big to be crossed by a bridge*, another week's ride brought Marco to Xi'an, the provincial capital of Shaanxi, but formerly the national capital of several dynasties. *Many good and valiant kings have reigned over it*, notes Marco, confusing the region and its past prominence with the idea that it is yet another kingdom. However, it is not all that surprising if Marco's knowledge of geography and history is confused, particularly considering the direction his mission would taken him. Once past Xi'an, his westward travels took him across the mountains into the Sichuan basin, then a second set of mountains into the foreign realms of Yunnan and Tibet. *They speak a language of their own*, writes Marco, *which is very difficult to understand*.[50] Perhaps it should only be expected that Marco should have never mastered Chinese, when one of his first trips within China took him into realms where

Chinese was useless to him, and where the Central Asian languages he had already mastered were far more beneficial.

Marco's trip to the south-west seems to have been rather uneventful for him, leading his narrative to head off on several doubtful tangents, as if to imply there was more action and excitement than there really was. Images of dragons on temple walls and the sight of crocodile skins for sale in marketplaces combined to inspire Marco with tales of *snakes and great serpents of such vast size as to strike fear into those who see them ...* , or so says an excitable Marco, without once stating outright that he has seen a live specimen for himself – crocodiles are not native to Yunnan, and any examples he saw were likely to have been imported across the mountains from Burma. *You may be assured that some of them are ten paces in length; some are more and some less. And in bulk they are equal to a great cask, for the bigger ones are about ten palms in girth* – a strangely exact description that, while it implies being able to measure a crocodile in person, also implies that the crocodile was so passive as to be dead already. *Their mouth is large enough to swallow a man whole, and is garnished with great teeth. And in short they are so fierce-looking and so hideously ugly that every man and beast must stand in fear and trembling of them.*[51]

Although Marco was in a place that is regarded as part of modern China, he had already passed beyond the borders of 'China' as it was known in his own time. The Yunnan region was known as the Dali kingdom, a separate ethnic and political region only co-opted into China by the Mongol conquest – no wonder the people's customs and speech confused Marco. In western Yunnan, Marco wrote that he had reached the kingdom of *Zardandan* – Persian for 'gold teeth', and thought to be a reference to the Dali locals' habit of wearing gold covers over their two front incisors. As with his references to most other places on his travel, his use of Persian terminology helps identify the language in which he learned much of his information about the places he saw.

Marco's description of the places and people of the regions he called Zardandan and Karajan, and even further south to Burma (Mien) and Bengal (Bengala), occasionally mix up dates and officials' names. Sometimes he describes the region as if it were part of Mongol territory, although in other occasions he is clearly referring to a region still subject to Mongol pacification. Such a mixed message suggests that Marco made several trips to the south-west during his years in China; trips which have been combined to make a single itinerary from Khanbalikh to the southwest in the final version of his narrative. It is likely that a similar series of trips, taken over the course of several years, formed the itinerary that followed Marco's description of the route on the other direction of the fork in the road, from Khanbalikh to the south-east, where Marco would spend substantially more time.

Cathay

Only such cities have been described as I, Marco, passed through on my journey through the province, leaving out those on either side and the intervening regions whose enumerations would be too tedious.[52] With these words, Marco stakes a bold claim in his book, that he is not simply recounting stories overheard from third parties or picked up from other books, but that he is recounting his direct experience. Strangely, however, this statement only appears in a small number of the more private manuscripts, and not in the more generally available edition.

It is difficult to determine precisely what role Marco may have played in the government of Khubilai Khan. He is not mentioned by any identifiable name in the records of the Yuan dynasty (the Mongol administration), but the Yuan chronicles are themselves remarkably reticent about racial origins of contemporary officials – perhaps an attempt to downplay the foreign nature of Mongol rule.

While Marco's racial origin would have been of little concern to the Mongols, he still may appear somewhere in the records of the Mongols. However, his book makes no claim of high office for its author, merely limiting its résumé of Marco to his role as some sort of emissary for Khubilai. The best clue to Marco's role in Khubilai's government was provided many years later in his last will and testament, which listed among his possessions *the silver belt of a Tartar knight*.[53] The choice of words, likely as they are to have been Marco's own, and using terminology in Italian that he himself regarded as a reasonable translation, become all the more intriguing when one compares them to Marco's use of the term 'knight' in his book.

In what may have been a reflection both of Marco's understanding of the term, and of Rustichello's romantic notion of chivalry, Marco's book appears to use the term 'knights' to translate the Mongol *keshigten* – the personal retainers of the Khan. Already numbering 10,000 by the time of Genghis Khan, with their numbers swelled by another several thousand during the time of Khubilai, each *keshig* wore a belt of office adorned with gold and silver thread, and enjoyed a ceremonial rank somewhere above that of a colonel – a commander of 1,000 men.

If Marco had been one of the *keshigten*, it would certainly explain both how he had enjoyed a position of some authority and also why he might never have risen to true prominence, if he was merely one in many thousand officials. But merely because the name 'Marco Polo' does not appear in the records of the Yuan dynasty, it does not necessarily follow that Marco was unmentioned. Like all other foreigners in Mongol employment, his name would have been transcribed and transposed into an alien script. It is much more likely that by the time Marco had adopted a Persian, Turkic or Mongol name by the time he reached China, or perhaps even a Chinese one. Such means of identification need not bear any resemblance

Giovanni Marignolli

Despite the visits of John of Plano Carpini, Marco's father and uncle and Marco himself, and many others, the only European to be officially acknowledged in the records of the Yuan dynasty is Giovanni Marignolli, a papal envoy who resided in Khanbalikh between 1342 and 1347. Even so, Marignolli is still not named, and only mentioned at all because of the nature of his gift to the Khan, a massive European warhorse, the likes of which the Mongols had not seen before. Nor is Marignolli correctly identified – his visit is simply listed as an embassy from 'the country of the Franks'.

to the pronunciation of his Christian name at all. If, in the modern world, 'Jonathan Clements' can somehow transform in Chinese to 'Cun Zheng', the chances of finding a 'Marco Polo' in Yuan records is remote indeed, even if he were mentioned directly.[54]

Marco's description of a single 'journey' from Khubilai's capital at Khanbalikh, down to the south-eastern port town of Quanzhou, seems to be another combination of several trips. The southern-most part of the itinerary is more confused, as if Marco had only visited the places once. Further to the north, his descriptions are highly detailed, as if he had spent prolonged periods in many of the towns, or made multiple visits.

It is here, for the first time, that Marco finds himself in China proper – the region once ruled by the Southern Song that Marco called Manzi or Cathay, rather than the northern regions of Khitai, which were still Chinese, but heavily influenced by generations of foreign rulers, including the departed Jin dynasty.

The Venetian trader's son was greatly impressed with the rich mercantile life of south China. The size of the Yangtze and Yellow Rivers, affording such deep inland access to large boats, was of great interest to him, as was their connection to each other by a mighty inland canal. *You must know*, writes Marco of the Yangtze, *that it is a mile in width. It is very deep, so that big ships can sail on it without difficulty. It teems with big fish and there are cities all along its banks. I am afraid to tell you how many ships there are on this river, for fear I should be called a liar.*[55]

Marco's comments on the canal system are particularly telling, since his descriptions of waterways and certain special dams and flows demonstrate that he saw several of these places for himself. More intriguingly, his narrative also reflects changing canal access during the period. Marco states, rightly, that a canal network linked Khanbalikh to the south – this much was true from 1285, although only with limited cargoes. But he also describes materials arriving in Khanbalikh as making the final leg of their journey in *cart-loads* – a revealing choice of words, since the waterways did not extend into Khanbalikh itself until 1293, the year after Marco left China. During his time in China, the final stage of a merchant's journey to the city would indeed have involved off-loading boats outside the city, and placing the cargo on carts for the last few miles. If, as some of his critics claim, he was using other peoples' writings as sources for his descriptions of the east, the sources he had were remarkably up to date.[56]

After the liberated, accommodating and, above all, available women of the Mongol north and non-Chinese border regions, Marco was taken aback by the relative seclusion of women in the south. Instead of breathless tales of easy sex, as found elsewhere in his travels, his private account of south Chinese girls reflect a very different culture. *You must know that the young ladies of the province of Cathay excel in modesty and the strict observance of decorum*, writes Marco. *They do not frisk and frolic and dance or fly into a pet. They do not keep watch at the windows gazing at passers-by or exposing themselves to their gaze. They do not offer a ready ear to improper stories. They do not gad about to parties and entertainments. If it happens that they go out to some respectable place ... they walk in the company of their mothers, not glancing brazenly about them but some of them wearing pretty hoods over their heads which obstruct their upward view. On the way, they always walk with their eyes cast down in front of their feet. In the presence of their elders they are respectful and never utter a needless word – indeed, they do not speak at all in their presence unless addressed ... and never listening to suitors.*[58]

Coal

Another of Marco's marvellous descriptions of the east included *a sort of black stone, which is dug out of veins in the hillsides and burns like logs. These stones keep a fire burning better than wood.*[57] Marco had stumbled across coal, apparently unknown in Italy at the time. It had become increasingly important in China during the Song dynasty, particularly as the swiftly growing demand for firewood had deforested the areas around the major cities of Kaifeng and Hangzhou.

One gets a sense, in Marco's description of the women of south China, of intense frustration masquerading as pious observation. After so many implications of earlier adventures among Persians, Uighurs, Tibetans and Dali women, he is reduced to long lists of all the things that Chinese girls will *not* do, ending with a prolonged and rather obsessive account of the local demand that girls marry as virgins.

Presumably solely on hearsay, Marco describes the ritual assessment of a bride's virginity by the elder women of the groom's family, and notes that the intact status of a hymen is not something that the Mongols would, or could place such emphasis on. *You must know that to ensure this strict preservation of virginity, the maidens always walk so daintily that they never advance one foot more than a finger's breadth beyond the other, since physical integrity is often destroyed by a wanton gait. This rule must be understood as applying {only} to the natives of Cathay. The Tartars do not trouble about such refinements, since their daughters and wives often go riding with them, so that it is quite credible that their integrity might be somewhat affected.*[59] Notably, the strange gait that Marco describes would also be the way that a woman would walk if her feet had been bound, hobbling from heel to heel as swiftly as possible – although Marco never mentions footbinding explicitly, he may have indirectly reported one of its side-effects.

While in south China, Marco took a much more direct interest in local religions, attending temples in person, while protesting a little too much about his lack of interest in the beliefs themselves. For his Christian readership back in Europe, he provides a dispassionate assessment of heathen superstitions. *Among the idolaters there are eighty-four idols, each with its own name. They declare that that the supreme god has assigned to each of these its own distinctive faculty, one concerned with the finding of lost objects, one with ensuring the fertility of the crops and tempering the weather for their growth, one with the safeguarding of flocks; and so with other activities, whether in prosperity or adversity.*[60] But Marco's description of Chinese native religion seems strangely exact – there are hundreds of local deities not the precise 84 he mentions, and his observation seems based upon a head-count of idols in a single temple.

Reading between the lines of Marco's narrative, and his particular interest in the deities of lost items, we can perhaps reconstruct his visit to a single temple, where an oracle of some description sat in permanent consultation. *If anyone has lost anything, either because he has been robbed or because he does not know where he left it … he will go … to the old woman, so that she may inquire of these idols about the missing object. She will then instruct him to offer incense to the idols. After this she will question them about the lost object, and they will reply as the case may be. Then she will say to the loser: 'Look in such-and-such a place and you will find it.' … And by this means, I, Marco, found a ring that I had lost – but not by making any offering to the idols or paying them homage.*[61]

As with the many other things unsaid in Marco's public manuscript, or even merely implied in the private version, the author dared not suggest to Christian readers that he had had any truck with non-Christian religions or proscribed practices. Marco did, however, note that believers who consulted the same oracle might also prevail upon her to put curses upon those who had wronged them. *If anyone has stolen anything from another, and on being admonished, refused to return it, then, if the thief is a woman, while she is handling a knife in the kitchen or in the course of some other task, she cuts her hand or stumbles into the fire, or some such misfortune befalls her; if the thief is a man, then in like manner while he is chopping wood he cuts his foot or he breaks an arm or a leg or some other part of his body.*[62] However, Marco makes no comment on whether he believes such superstitions himself, as to do so would have invited censure from pious readers.

Marco's account of south China includes multiple references to another marvel, albeit one that seems prosaic to modern readers

– paper money. Paper itself was a relatively recent innovation back in Europe, having only been introduced by Arabs in the 12th century. Italy's first paper mill was only established shortly before Marco left for the east, and so he must have been all the more surprised to find such a new-fangled invention already established in China for use in books, paintings and, most shockingly to a European audience, money. Time and again in his travels, Marco refers to 'the Khan's paper money', associating a thousand-year-old Chinese invention with the new Mongol aristocracy. In far-flung regions, such as Tibet, he notes paper money by its absence, since natives still deal with each other by barter, or by local currencies based on precious metals, cowrie shells or salt blocks. But in south China, almost every city is identified as being a place where paper money is used, partly because Marco seems taken with the novelty, but largely because the use of such a currency, backed only by the promise of the Mongol ruler to redeem it, was a sure sign that Khubilai's rule was accepted and unquestioned by the bulk of China's mercantile population.

It was only once Marco was in the realm of the south China that he began to collect stories of the Song dynasty, so recently conquered by the Mongols. Unsurprisingly, Marco's version of the fall of south China contains elements of historical events, but combines several historical figures, and filters the entire story through the ideas and attitudes of the victors.

Marco clearly did not hear the story in Chinese. He refers to the last great 'king' of south China as *Facfur*, a Persian variant of the Arabic *Baghbur*, meaning Son of Heaven. *He took great delight in women*, writes Marco, *and was beneficent to the poor. In his province he had no horses.*[63] This last is patently untrue, but a reasonable reflection of the attitude displayed by the nomadic, equestrian Mongols to the people of south China. The stories that Marco heard about Facfur did not seem malicious in any way – as one might expect of collaborators in the company of an emissary of the conquering power, everyone Marco met seemed to have nothing but fond reminiscences about their former ruler. Facfur, says Marco, was rich beyond measure, able to adopt thousands of abandoned children as fosterlings, and so kind-hearted that he had been known to build a great house for a poor man, so that a pauper's dwelling would not suffer by comparison with his rich neighbours. Such nonsensical fables seem carefully calculated to imply that the former rulers of the south Chinese were rich but somewhat stupid.

The Hundred Eyes

Bayan (c.1235–95) was a high-ranking official in the Mongol administration, first finding fame as a military leader in Khubilai's invasion of the Dali kingdom in 1253. By 1265, he had risen to the position of *Chingsang*, or Secretary of State in Khubilai's administration. He was later a leading figure in the conquest of southern China. Following the appointment of Khubilai's son Nomukhan as a Central Asian governor, and the boy's subsequent kidnapping, the aging Bayan was dispatched as the leader of a rescue force, but recalled when he failed to achieve much. Marco refers to him in his original text as *Baian Cingsan*. Coincidentally, *Bai-yan*, in Chinese, means 'one hundred eyes'.

When Marco turns once more to the tale of the conquest of the south, he makes it clear how swiftly the southlands fell to the Mongol conquerors. The famous general Bayan pushed ever southward, not stopping to besiege those towns that resisted him, secure in the knowledge that Mongol reinforcements were close behind him. Instead, Bayan beat a path straight for Hangzhou, the Song capital, where Facfur's widowed queen awaited. Here, as elsewhere Marco confuses the widow of one emperor with the mother of his successor, perhaps understandably since there were two 'queens' of the south in many accounts, but only one woman was brought to Khanbalikh as hostage of Khubilai. As Marco tells it, the surrender of the south Chinese was assured by an ancient prophecy, that when the young emperor's regent heard the name 'Hundred-eyes', she called to mind the prediction of the astrologers that a man who had a hundred eyes would rob them of their kingdom. Thereupon, she surrendered to Bayan.[64]

It seems that Marco had a good reason for his interest in the history of Hangzhou. As the former Song capital, the town had an important position in the infrastructure of south China, as the nexus of roads, the centre of waterways and the home of a large population. As one of the last Song cities to fall, Hangzhou was not part of the first census of the Mongol empire conducted in the 1250s, nor of the earliest Mongol census of China, conducted in 1271. However, Hangzhou was subjected to a careful audit soon after its surrender, as the Yuan dynasty chronicles put it, 'to record the number and quantity of its soldiers, people, money and grain'.[65] As for Marco, he was present during the compilation of the data, in an unknown capacity, since his book notes that *Messer Marco found himself in this city ... when account was being rendered to the Great Khan's agents of its total revenue and population.*[66] He was thus able to present a highly detailed report of the former Chinese capital, quoting chapter and verse on its riches, although the city as he described it was regarded by many of his later European readers as an impossible fiction.

The Finest City in the World

Marco was awestruck by the size and magnificence of the former Chinese capital, Hangzhou. *It well merits a description,* he writes, *because it is without doubt the finest and most splendid city in the world.*[67] Nor was Marco's affection for the city limited to his own experience – beyond Marco's own love of the town's canals, taverns and womenfolk, he also reports that it was Khubilai Khan's best city, not for what it was, but for the income it generated. *To speak the truth,* writes Marco, *this part {of China} is the greatest and most productive; and because of the great revenue that the Great Khan derives from it, it is his favourite province, and he takes all the more care to watch it well, and to keep the people contented.*[68]

Hangzhou had not always been so impressive. A walled fort established around AD 600, it was little more than a hot, damp provincial town until transport networks brought it a new-found prominence. Hangzhou sat on the coast of China halfway on the long journey between the cosmopolitan port of Canton in the south, and the outlying sea-ports that could take goods inland to Khanbalikh. It also sat at the southern end of the Grand Canal, that incredible waterway that stretched all the way to Khanbalikh itself, linking Hangzhou to the Yellow River, the Yangtze, and all points in between. From AD 1000 onwards, Hangzhou had been one of the major centres not merely of domestic trade, but also of China's connections to other lands – Japan to the east, Indo-China and India to the south, and thence to the Arab world, and the far, far west of Marco's Europe.

The town gained another boost in 1126, when the Jurchen barbarians of the Jin captured the former Chinese capital Kaifeng from the Northern Song dynasty. Several cities were considered as a replacement capital, before the first emperor of the Southern Song, a half-brother of the emperor who had been captured at the fall of Kaifeng, was established in Hangzhou. Officially, Hangzhou was selected because the other candidates were too open to attack, although the fact it was the emperor's mother's hometown may have also had some bearing on the decision. To make it clear that the city was only a stop-gap measure while the Song dynasty dealt with the usurpers in the north, the city was officially known as *Xingzai-suo*, or 'the place of temporary residence'. It is this term, misheard as Kinsai or Quinsai, which Marco uses to describe the city throughout his book.

Thanks to its newfound status as an interim capital, Hangzhou's size was increased by new arrivals, so that its population at the time of Marco's arrival would have been over a million inhabitants. Marco himself claimed that the city contained 1.6 million hearths, although such a large number is likely to have referred to both Hangzhou and its outer environs, rather than the smaller walled city proper.

However, even though Marco claims to have spent much time in Hangzhou, some of his description of it still seems, if not second-hand, then at least mangled in translation. He erroneously claims that the nearby West Lake is 30 leagues long, whereas such dimensions describe the West Lake *district*, not the actual body of water which it borders. He also takes literally, perhaps owing to a loss in translation, his guide's use of typical hyperbole – when Marco says there are 'twelve thousand bridges', he seems to be duped by the Chinese use of 'ten thousand' as a number considered close to infinity.

Marco paints a picture of a city under constant surveillance, and twice implies that this is typical not merely of Hangzhou during the Mongol census, but of all cities in occupied China. *You must know that all the townsfolk of this city ... have the following custom. Each one has written on the door of his house his own name and his wife's and those of his sons and his sons' wives and his slaves and all the occupants of the house, and how many horses he possesses ... In this way, the governor of every city is kept informed about all the people who live in it.*[69]

He also assumed, perhaps rightly, that his stays at Hangzhou taverns were typical of the experience of all travellers in the Mongol world. *All those who keep inns or provide lodgings for travellers write down the names of all those who lodge with them and the dates of their stay. So throughout the year the Great Khan can know who is coming and going throughout his dominions. And this is a useful piece of knowledge to prudent statesmen.*[70]

The Whale

Marco usually avoided mention of 'marvels' or unlikely happenings, but was impressed enough with the evidence of one such occurrence to report it faithfully. A 'great fish', actually a whale, ran ashore in Hangzhou, *full 100 paces long, but its girth was by no means proportionate to its length.* Some townsfolk ate the flesh of the 'fish', but *many of those who did so died.*[71] Marco did not witness the incident itself, but he saw the head of the 'fish' in a local temple. His story has since been backed up by Yuan dynasty chronicles.

Variant texts of Marco differ in their attitudes towards Hangzhou. He notes, perhaps with some scepticism, that *it was stated that the city ... is about 100 miles in circumference*, although the outer walls of contemporary Hangzhou were only about 23 miles around – or 70 Chinese *li*. Adding 30 *li* of outer suburbs, and then mixing one's units of measure would give us Marco's muddled version. His neutral, and truthful comments that the city was crisscrossed by canals were augmented

in some Venetian editions by the words 'like Venice', implying that this large mercantile city of island wards and bridges reminded him of home. But Hangzhou's waterways had a different origin to those of Venice. Although Marco may not have realised, the

This 19th-century image of Guangzhou (Canton) perhaps resembles the canals of Hangzhou in Polo's time.

channels through the city were part of an extensive network that not only permitted waterborne transport, but also brought fresh water down from the nearby West Lake. With architecture chiefly comprising wooden houses, the canals also served as firebreaks during the height of summer, and sources of water in case of fire. Nor is Hangzhou the ideal candidate to resemble Venice – in the China or Marco Polo's day, nearby Suzhou had a canal network that bore a far closer likeness to medieval Venice.

When it comes to direct experience, Marco seems far more taken with the girls of Hangzhou, particularly the prostitutes *whose number is so great that I do not venture to state it. These are not confined to the neighbourhood of the squares – the quarter usually assigned to them – but are to be found throughout the city, attired with great magnificence, heavily perfumed, attended by many handmaids and lodged in richly ornamented apartments.*

Marco's comments echo other surviving accounts from the period, which rated the courtesans of Hangzhou as the most beautiful in China, and noted that local restaurants employed beautiful 'singing girls' to entice customers in to restaurants, wait on their tables, and suggest expensive dishes to the gullible in order to hike up their bill. Hangzhou was notable in the late Song, and also in the early Yuan dynasty, for its large numbers of state prostitutes. With the population swelled by refugees and relocated soldiers from the fallen north, much of the town's revenue had derived from a local tax on alcohol, leading many of the bar-girls to work on a commission, charged with pushing whatever commodities gained them the best return from the lonely military men who flocked to them. Such patterns of consumption and behaviour seem to have continued into Marco's time, with Hangzhou's position as a national entrepôt making much of its life and commerce revolve around luxuries and entertainments, even in the wake of a crushing defeat and invasion by foreign invaders. The result was a large service economy of entertainers, singers, bookmakers and the organisers of sporting events worth betting on in the first place

Mission from the East

While Marco settled in China, two subjects of Khubilai Khan made a remarkable journey in the opposite direction. Rabban Sauma and Rabban Mark, two Nestorian monks of Uighur ethnic origin made a joint mission to Europe using funds appropriated from Khubilai's son and nephew. They followed the Silk Road back to Jerusalem, where Mark was eventually created Metropolitan Patriarch – 'archbishop', in the Nestorian faith. As an agent of Arghun, the ruler of Persia, Sauma went on to travel Europe as far as Bordeaux, where the English king Edward I received communion from him. Sauma died in Baghdad in 1294.

– Marco called Hangzhou 'the city of heaven', but it seems more likely that for a tired diplomat returning from prolonged trips in the hinterland, it was a city of fun.

A Chinese text, written in 1274, noted one tavern in the area with 'a dozen prostitutes, luxuriously dressed and heavily made-up, [gathered] at the entrance of the main arcade to await the command of customers, [with] an airy gracefulness like that of the Immortals'.[72] Marco himself, as usual, without once claiming to have known such details first-hand, noted that the *ladies are highly proficient and accomplished in the uses of endearments and caresses, with words suited and adapted to every sort of person, so that foreigners who have once enjoyed them remain utterly beside themselves and so captivated by their sweetness and charm that they can never forget them.*[73]

His other chief interest in Hangzhou was that of a tourist, examining the sites of the departed Song dynasty, particularly *the palace of the fugitive king*. Hangzhou, like many other Chinese capitals throughout history, once included an inner bastion or 'forbidden city' accessible only to the imperial household – as in Khanbalikh to the north, there was an imperial palace, attached to large walled hunting park. *Sometimes, the King would set the girls a-coursing after ... game with dogs, and when they were tired they would head to the groves that overhung the lakes, and leaving their clothes there they would come forth naked and enter the water and swim about ... whilst it was the King's desire to watch them ... Sometimes the King would have his dinner carried to those groves, which were dense with lofty trees, and there be waited on by those young ladies. And thus he passed his life in this constant dalliance with women, without so much as knowing what arms* [i.e. war] *meant. And the result of all this cowardice and effeminacy was that he lost his dominion to the Great Khan in that base and shameful way that you have heard.*[74]

Marco paints a melancholy picture of wandering through the dilapidated remains of the Song dynasty's great citadel, forced to imagine how the gold must have looked on the roof, and how the chatter of a thousand handmaids had assailed the ears. He is, however, largely unsympathetic to the travails of the Song dynasty itself, commenting on several occasions that the opulent life of Hangzhou had caused its inhabitants to neglect their responsibilities to arm, train and prepare to defend their land. Strangely, even though Marco has admiringly described a very similar hunting ground, pleasure garden and relaxation routine in Khubilai's own capital to the north, his tales of forest picnics and swimming trips in Hangzhou is used as an example of the degenerate and decadent nature of the Song, and a sign that their downfall had been long overdue.

All this account was given to me by a rich merchant of Kinsai whom I encountered in the city, a man of ripe years who had been intimately acquainted with King Facfur and knew all about his life, and had seen the palace in all its glory. He undertook to conduct me through it. The pavilions in front, being occupied by the Great Khan's viceroy, are just as they used to be. But the chambers of the damsels have all fallen in ruin, and only vestiges of them remain. Likewise the wall that encircled the groves and gardens has fallen to the ground, and neither trees nor animals are left.[75]

In the Khan's Service

Even though Marco's book is not specifically a biography, but rather a 'Description of the World', it remains remarkably reticent about its author's career during the years he spent in the Far East. Apart from asides in the journeys to and from China, there is little mention of Marco's uncle and father, who were presumably in his company at least some of the time. Nor is there much concerning Marco's status – the possibility that he was a *keshig*, or Mongol knight, has been inferred rather than implied. Several variant texts of his book, although notably not the ones usually regarded as the most trustworthy, comment that Marco enjoyed a very high administrative position in the city of Yangzhou, somewhat to the north of Hangzhou, on the other side of the Yangtze river and some distance up the Grand Canal. *Messer Marco himself, who is the subject of this book*, comments one edition, *governed this city for three years.*[76]

The records of the Yuan dynasty beg to differ, offering no governor's name in the period Marco was in China that could conceivably be a Venetian *semuren*. But even if Marco's claim is a vain boast, based perhaps on a far lowlier position, his choice of location is an intriguing one. In generations after his eventual return from Asia, Yangzhou would gain a small but significant population of Italian merchants, established enough to marry and raise children in their new home. Much of what we know about this population of *semuren* comes from two gravestones, discovered in Yangzhou in 1951, belonging to one Caterina (d.1342) and her brother Antonio (d.1344), children of Domenico Ilioni or Vilioni, a Genoese merchant living in China at the time. Notably, the extant records of Yangzhou, be it for tax, census or simple reportage, contain no record whatsoever either of the Ilioni family or any other foreigners in town, even though Yangzhou even boasted a Franciscan convent during the 1320s. If Marco's prolonged stay in Yangzhou similarly slipped beneath the notice of contemporary record keepers, then perhaps he did enjoy a more prominent position in Yangzhou than current evidence supports. But there may be a simpler explanation, that early editions of his text reported a simple *sejourna* (sojourn) in Yangzhou, which was somehow corrupted by copyists in France into a *seigneurie* (lordship) there.[77]

Possibly, Marco's role in Khubilai's China was in a profession that would not have gained him the sympathies of his Christian readership. With Khubilai Khan still prevaricating about his religious allegiances, there was still a chance that the Mongols might return to plague Europe once more – if Marco had spent 20 years in their military service, as an adviser, strategist and collaborator, then his reception back in a Europe still under Mongol threat would have been decidedly cooler.

But Marco took a great, some might say a professional, interest in military matters. Many modern editions reduce or drop entirely many of his discussions of Mongol wars, pleading that Marco's book is foremost an account of marvellous beasts and fantastic countries, and that endless, repetitive narrations of long-forgotten conflicts offer nothing of substance to a modern readership. And yet, someone involved in the compilation of Marco's book took a keen interest in warfare. We might imagine Rustichello, tiring of yet another discourse on salt manufacture, town guilds or strange vegetables, pleading with his co-author to come up with a diverting tangent of stabbings and battle-cries, if only for a couple of pages – another juicy murder, perhaps, like the tale of Ahmad in Khanbalikh.

A Chinese watercolour of Khubilai Khan.

However, it seems unlikely that Marco's notes on military affairs had such superficial origins. In what may have been a natural reflection of his years of service to an invading power in an occupied territory, military concerns occupy a substantial part of his book – a full sixth of the unabridged manuscript is devoted to Khubilai's wars, chiefly with other Mongols. Perhaps even more suspiciously, Marco mentions hardly anyone by name who is not directly involved in military matters. For the Mongols, whose entire administrative apparatus was geared for war, this is unsurprising, but Marco mentions few Chinese in his text – in fact, apart from a few folktales about 'King Facfur' and his defeated nobles in the south, the only Chinese that Marco identifies are two generals and a colonel. It seems a remarkably low count of local acquaintances to show for 20 years in a foreign country, although of course, Marco mentions many more *semuren* associates – Persians and Central Asian Muslims, many of whom were fellow servants of the Mongol administration.

Mangonel

A mangonel (from the Greek: *magga-non*, 'war engine') was a type of siege weapon, referred to in some editions of Marco's book also as a *trebuchet*. A sling or bowl at one end of a long arm would hurl rocks or other missiles for long distances. The need for a firm base and the difficulty of precise aiming reduced their usefulness in battles, although they were often used in sieges, where attackers could sustain long bombardments on random targets among the defenders. It was sometimes referred to by soldiers as a 'scorpion', for the flick of its tail-like delivery system, or the 'mule' for the kick it delivered.

At one point in Marco's text, he openly claims that he spent at least some time in the Khan's military service, at the siege of the Chinese city of Xiangyang. With the Mongols unable to completely surround the city, provisions continued to arrive to help the defenders, prolonging the siege for three years after hostilities first began.

The Great Khan had sent back word that take it they must, and find a way how. Then spoke up the two brothers and Messer Marco the son, and said; 'Great Prince, we have with us among our followers men who are able to construct mangonels which shall cast such great stones that they garrison will never be able to stand them, but will surrender ... ' And they had two men among their followers, a German and a Nestorian Christian, who were masters of that business, and these they directed to construct two or three mangonels, each of which cast stones of 300 lbs.[78]

As Marco tells it, he and his associates were able to provide two or three of the dreaded siege engines, along with 60 large rocks. As they began lobbing them into the town, the panicking citizens swiftly surrendered. *And all this came about through the exertions of Messer Niccolo, Messer Maffeo and Messer Marco; and it was no small matter.*

The passage, however, is highly suspect. In a book into which Marco rarely inserts himself as an actual participant, and which hardly mentions his father and uncle at all, it repeats all three of their names four times in less than a page. Moreover, Marco cannot possibly have been in the area at the time. The historical siege at Xiangyang did take place, in a very similar fashion to that described by Marco, but in 1273, before Marco had even arrived in China. Both Persian and Chinese accounts of the Mongol conquest admit that the fall of Xiangyang was brought about with the assistance of foreign engineers, but credit altogether different individuals. Rashid al-Din's *History of the Mongols*, for example, praises 'Talib the mangonel maker from Ba'albek and Damascus, with his sons Abu Bakr, Ibrahim and Mohammed' for their engineering abilities, with not a German or Italian in sight.[79]

Marco's book is far more accurate and less boastful in the matter of internal struggles among the Mongol ruling family. In the case of one conflict, between Khubilai, his cousin Khaidu and uncle Nayan, Marco actually provides greater detail than the chronicles of the Mongol administration itself.

Although many years had elapsed since the succession disputes concerning Khubilai's elevation to Great Khan, bitter feelings still ran below the surface among the Mongol aristocracy. The family of Genghis Khan's eldest son had been edged out a generation earlier, and now brooded in the far west, on the borders of Europe, where they were expected to win further victories, but in fact had largely given up. Meanwhile, Khubilai had obtained the rank of Great Khan at the expense of another strand of the family – the

The 'elephant castle' from which Khubilai Khan commanded the battle against the rebellious Nayan in 1287.

descendants of the third son of Genghis Khan. As noted earlier, these had been originally appeased through the appointment of Khaidu as the viceroy of the Mongol homeland. There, Khaidu regarded himself as the true inheritor of the destiny of Genghis Khan, leading to series of skirmishes and conflicts in inner Asia.

In one of Khaidu's intrigues, he struck a deal with Nayan,

another disaffected member of Khubilai's family, then ruling the region later known as Manchuria. The warlords agreed a two-pronged assault in 1287, with Khaidu attacking Khubilai from the west, and Nayan rising up in revolt in the east. However, since Khaidu was in a state of constant conflict with Khubilai anyway, the upshot really only concerned Nayan's actions. Nayan raised an army and marched on Khubilai.

When the Great Khan heard what was afoot, he made his preparations in right good heart, like one who feared not the issue of an attempt so contrary to justice. Confident of his own conduct and prowess, he was in no degree disturbed, but vowed he would never wear crown again if he brought not those two traitorous and disloyal Tartar chiefs to an ill end.[80]

Khubilai Khan personally led the army that suppressed Nayan's rebellion, dragging himself out of retirement and drafting his personal retinue to fight on his behalf. With other Mongol troops unable to leave their posts elsewhere in the Empire for fear of further uprisings, Khubilai instead leaned on the *keshigten* and retainers in the immediate neighbourhood. *In fact*, exclaims Marco with considerable glee, *those 360,000 horsemen that he got together consisted merely of the falconers and whippers-in that were about the court!* – a troop levy that also gave Khubilai the benefit of surprise. *Now the Great Khan arrived so fast and so suddenly that the others knew nothing of the matter. For the Khan had caused such strict watch to be made in every direction for scouts that every one that appeared was instantly captured. Thus Nayan had no warning of his coming, and was completely taken by surprise; insomuch as when the Great Khan's army came up, he was asleep in the arms of a wife of his of whom he was extravagantly fond ...* [81]

When the day of battle dawned, the Great Khan suddenly appeared on a mound that rose from the plain where Nayan's forces were bivouacked... {Nayan's men} felt so secure that they had posted no sentries around their camp and sent out no patrols to the van or rear. {Khubilai Khan} stood on top of a wooden tower, full of crossbowmen and archers, which was carried by four elephants wearing stout leather armour draped with cloths of silk and gold.[82]

Nayan's men were taken by surprise, and rushed to gather their weapons and armour while Khubilai patiently waited. The two armies then joined in a battle which Marco describes in impressive detail – might he have been personally present? The Toledo manuscript and some others add elements that would have both tantalised and dismayed Marco's European readers. *Now you must know that Nayan was a baptised Christian, and bore the cross on his banner.*[83]

Legends of Marco's day held that during a civil war in Rome in AD 312, the Emperor Constantine claimed to have had a vision of the Christian *chi-rho* symbol (a cross-like merging of the first two letters of 'Christ' in Greek), with the message 'In this Sign You will Conquer' *–In Hoc Signo Vinces*. Legend has it that Constantine made the cross his standard at the battle of Milvian Bridge, defeating his rival in the conflict. He was then believed to have converted to Christianity, becoming the first Christian emperor, although it is perhaps fairer to say that he merely decriminalised the religion, only converting on his deathbed. However, to Marco's readership, the thought of a Mongol general carrying a cross into battle would have raised high hopes for conversions among the Mongols, and dashed them again as the battle ended in Nayan's defeat.

Nayan's supposed conversion had been a pragmatic move. His claim to have been baptised would have helped encourage local soldiers to flock to his cause. It would have also politicised religion in a way that Khubilai had steadfastly tried to avoid. Whereas Khubilai famously steered a diplomatic course between Chinese traditionalists, Muslims, Buddhists and Christians at his court, Nayan's use of the crucifix as a battle-standard all but turned his rebellion into a crusade against Khubilai. One Marco manuscript tersely notes that Nayan's army 'included countless Christians, who were all killed.'[84] It is not clear from the meagre evidence whether this is a simple statement of severe casualties, or an economy of truth regarding sweeping Mongol reprisals – the massacre of every Christian who had dared to question Khubilai's authority.

The use of a Christian standard certainly presented enough of an issue for it to become the subject of post-battle arguments. *And after the Great Khan had conquered Nayan, as you have heard, it came to pass that the different kinds of people who were present, Saracens and Idolaters and Jews, and many others that believed not in God, did taunt those who were Christians because of the cross that Nayan had borne on his standard ... Thus they would say to the Christians: 'See now what precious help this God's Cross of yours has rendered Nayan, who was a Christian and a worshipper ... ' And such a din arose about the matter that it reached the Great Khan's own ears.*[85]

Keen to avoid religious conflict among his subjects, Khubilai was swift to quell such antagonism. He managed this in an impressive manner that combined the brutish common sense of Mongol tradition with the Chinese attitude towards a Mandate of Heaven and the medieval sense of trial by combat.

'If the Cross had rendered no help to Nayan,' Marco reports Khubilai as saying, *'in that it had done right well. Nor could that which was good, as it was, have done otherwise. For Nayan was a disloyal and traitorous rebel against his lord, and well deserved that which had befallen him ... . the Cross of your God did well in that it gave him no help against the right.'*[86] In other words, merely carrying a crucifix would not be enough to secure victory, one also had to be pure of heart – a concept that would have appealed not only to Christian readers, but to Marco's co-author Rustichello, with his long track record in Arthurian legend.

Absent and all but forgotten from Marco's account of the battle is the shadowy figure behind it all. If Khaidu had truly planned on mounting a campaign of his own in support of Nayan, his ambitions melted away, at least temporarily. Khaidu would continue to harass Khubilai in Inner Asia, and would outlive his great enemy, only to die in 1301 in the midst of yet another scuffle for power. Although Khubilai's forces fought many campaigns against Khaidu throughout the period that Marco was in China, Marco has far less to say about them, further implying that the richness of detail he offers on the battle with Nayan could have been based on personal experience.

The Death of Kings

Nayan's fate was that reserved by the Mongols for all victims believed to be of noble birth. Since the spilling of noble blood was not permitted in Mongol tradition, Nayan was instead rolled up in a carpet and trampled to death. Other Mongol methods of execution included strangulation with bowstrings. Unwanted babies were sometimes drowned in milk. Marco also reported that one of the leaders of the failed 1274 attack on Japan was left on a deserted island with his hands bound with buffalo hide – a cruel method of ensuring slow starvation.

However, while Marco had little to say about Khaidu himself, he, or his collaborator Rustichello, or quite possibly both of them were far more interested in a particular member of Khaidu's family. Marco was taken with the story of Khaidu's daughter Aiyaruk (Mongol: 'Bright Moon'), a warrior-woman whose name is also recorded as Khutulun in some other contemporary sources. *This damsel was very beautiful, but also so strong and brave that in all her father's realm there was no man who could outdo her in feats of strength. In all trials she showed greater strength than any man of them. Her father often desired to give her in marriage, but she would none of it. She vowed she would never marry till she found a man who could vanquish her in every trial; him she would wed and none else.*[87]

While Marco's account might sound far-fetched, or perhaps a faithful report of propaganda put about to improve Khaidu's credentials as an old-fashioned Mongol brawler (since even his little girl could break heads!), the story is confirmed in enough alternate accounts to have a shred of truth. Aiyaruk made it known that she would marry any man who could beat her in a wrestling match, but that if she won, her opponent would be required to forfeit a hundred horses.

By Marco's reckoning, Aiyaruk's victories had won her 10,000 horses by 1280, including a thousand obtained in a single bout with a proud princeling.

He came full confidently, and brought with him 100 horses at a single stroke ... King Khaidu and the Queen his wife ... greatly desired this prince for their daughter, seeing what a noble youth he was and the son of a great king. But the damsel answered that never would she let herself be vanquished if she could help it.[88]

Marco's readership would have been reared on classical legends of Amazons from the east, and may have been likely to expect some romantic denouement in which Aiyaruk gave herself to her valiant challenger, or some tragic climax in which she died resisting. Instead, Marco's story has no real finale; Aiyaruk simply beats her latest challenger, and he heads off embarrassed, while Aiyaruk goes on to become a renowned warrior in her father's entourage. *And gladly he took her, for not a knight in all his train played such feats of arms as she did. Sometimes she would quit her father's side and make a dash*

Amazons

The Amazons were a mythical tribe of women, thought in Classical antiquity to live in somewhere in Scythia – now Mongol territory. Their name appears to have been a translation error – the proto-Iranian word **ha-mazan* meaning 'warrior', somehow corrupted in the telling to the Greek *a-mazos* ('without [one] breast) or *a-masos* ('not touching [men]'). This led in turn to legends of fierce warrior women, whose initiation ceremony involved the cutting off of one breast to facilitate drawing a bow. Their most famous characters included Hippolyta, bride of Theseus, the axe-wielding Aella, Penthesilea the sometime enemy of Achilles and the legendary Thalestris, who supposedly challenged Alexander the Great to single combat.

at the host of the enemy, and seize some man ... as deftly as a hawk pounces on a bird, and carry him to her father; and this she did many a time.[89]

However, the most crucial military matter in Marco's book concerned a story that presented the Mongols in a far less favourable light. In describing a military failure that occurred during his residence in China, Marco would inadvertently inspire generations of explorers to go in search of an island that was not mentioned in Europe before his time: the land of the rising sun.

Cipangu

Like the 'Marco Polo Bridge', a minor element of Marco's narrative that found unexpected fame because of later events, his account of the distant eastern isle of 'Cipangu' was more influential and important than he could have ever suspected. The island, just off the coast of China, is the easternmost place he mentions in his book, according to him, some '1,500 miles' from the mainland.

Marco's 'Cipangu' was later identified with Japan, and his brief notes on it the first time that the island's existence had even been mentioned outside East Asia. Marco is unlikely to have ever visited Japan in person, but his interest in it reflects that of the Mongols themselves, since Japan remained the last known region in the East to be officially unconquered. The first that the Mongols heard about it came after their conquest of Korea, where they noted that Japanese pirates had taken advantage of the Mongol invasion to plunder the Korean coast. It was only when the Mongol occupation of Korea was complete, in the 1260s, that the Japanese pirate raids ceased – quite possibly because the raiders feared reprisals.

On the basis of Marco's account, the mysterious, militarily independent, treasure-laden island of Cipangu made its way onto late medieval maps, and became a favoured target for later explorers hoping to reach the 'Indies' by sailing west across the Atlantic. At least part of the land's appeal to later readers may have come from the emphasis Marco placed on treasure. One of

Japan's major exports during the Song dynasty had been gold and pearls, although many of Marco's claims may have dated solely from propaganda of the invasion years. *The people are white, civilised, and well favoured. They are Idolaters, and are dependent on nobody. And I can tell you the quantity of gold they have is endless ... they also have pearls in abundance, which are of a rose colour, but fine, big and round, and quite as valuable as the white ones. In this Island some of the dead are buried, and others are burnt. When a body is burnt they put one of these pearls in the mouth, for such is their custom.*[90]

In 1266, Khubilai had sent emissaries to Japan to announce that he was the new Emperor of China, and that Japan should offer tribute. As the closest point between Japan and the mainland, Korea was the natural point of departure for the ambassadors, but they never quite made it. Instead, they were dissuaded by Koreans, unwilling to involve themselves in a dispute between the Mongols and Japan, since the combat zone would very likely be Korea itself. When a new diplomatic mission finally reached Japan in 1268, it was plunged into a mess of contradictory responsibilities and authorities. The nominal ruler of Japan was the Emperor, but he was merely a puppet of the Shogun ('barbarian-quelling-general'), a military leader whose very job description precluded any pretence of making a deal with the Mongols. During this period, the Shogun was himself a puppet of the 'Shogun Regent', a hereditary office that held the true power. The new Shogun Regent, Hojo Tokimune,

Hojo Tokimune (1251–84)

The son of the late Shogun Regent Tokiyori, Hojo Tokimune was marginalised as a child after his father's death. His gradual rise through the ranks of the Shogunate was suddenly accelerated by the threat of the Mongols – his predecessor resigned over the refusal of the Japanese to send a reply to Khubilai, causing Tokimune to be promoted to Shogun Regent at the age of just 17. He oversaw the defences at Hakata Bay, and his associations with Buddhist monasteries led to him taking some of the credit for the *kamikaze*. He remains a hero in Japan to this day.

The Japanese defeat the Mongol invasion.

was a teenage boy who boldly sent the ambassadors home without a response at all – one was drafted, but never sent.

Several further attempts at contact met with no response, leading Khubilai to divert a small force from the ongoing conquest of China in 1274, around the time that Marco first arrived in China. Marco, however, does not regard Khubilai's designs on Japan as part of the overall Mongol conquest, instead suggesting that Khubilai was solely motivated by a desire for the legendary wealth of Japan. *{Khubilai} having heard much of the immense wealth that was in this island, formed a plan to get possession of it. For this reason he sent two of his barons with a great navy, and a great force of horse and foot.*[91]

The Japanese, however, had already determined that only one harbour in south Japan was large enough to hold a fleet. Tokimune's samurai forces were waiting on the shoreline for the Mongols, who were unable to disembark their full force at once, and eventually succumbed to a great storm that sunk many of the troop ships before they could even offload their crucial cargoes.

Estimates of Mongol losses in the great storm range as high as 13,000 — a military disaster for the troops who had surged so swiftly across the rest of Asia. In Japan, the intervention of the weather at a moment of dire peril was regarded as a sign that the gods themselves were prepared to protect Japan from foreign invaders, and had, allegedly, answered the prayers of many monasteries in Japan. The gods, argued Tokimune and his supporters, had shielded the Japanese with the aid of a 'divine wind' — the origin of the term *kamikaze*. The concept was stirring enough for the Japanese to behave with even greater bravado in 1275, when a new embassy arrived from Khubilai, asking them if they had learned their lesson. Instead, the ambassadors were executed, guaranteeing that a punitive expedition would be sent against Japan, at a date to be determined.

Kamikaze

The term Kamikaze achieved much greater notoriety in the 20th century, when it was applied to the pilots of suicide planes in the last-ditch defence of Japan from Allied forces. The word, however, was not originally used by the Japanese, who preferred to read the characters for 'Divine Wind' Chinese-style as *Shinpu*, as in the military unit Shinpu Special Attack Force. The characters were misread as 'kamikaze' by American translators, and the appellation has stuck to this day. In 1944 as in 1274, the implication of the Divine Wind was that Japan would be protected by the gods themselves in its time of direst military need.

Beforehand, Khubilai needed to subjugate the Southern Song, mop up several areas of resistance, and allow the Koreans some time to recover, since the peninsula was badly ravaged during the Mongol conquest and the subsequent preparations for the first expedition.

Whether or nor Marco was working in a directly military capacity, he seems to have been witness to the preparations for the second assault on Japan. In order to avoid the economic ruin of Korea, Khubilai spread preparations out all along the coastal ports of China. Even then, local officials complained that Khubilai's preparations were cripplingly expensive – a minister in Fujian noted that it had taken all his people's efforts to build and supply 50 ships, even though Khubilai had called on his district to provide four times as many.

At the time of assembly, two fleets set sail, one from Korea, and one from China. Marco describes 15,000 ships on the Yangtze river, *all belonging to the Great Khan and available to carry his armies to the isles of the sea; for I must tell you that the sea is a mere day's journey from this place. Each transport ship has a crew of twenty and carries about fifteen horses with the riders and provisions.*[92] Many apparent 'errors' in his account make more sense when one filters them through the attitudes of invading soldiers – Japan is not '1,500 miles' from the mainland; at its closest point it is more like 150 miles, although it is 1,500 Chinese *li* from Hangzhou, from where many of the troop ships were stocked and dispatched.

Internal strife led to difficulties in managing the multi-racial force. The division from Korean tired of waiting for the reinforcements from China, and set out without them, only to find that in the years since the first invasion attempt, the Japanese had fortified the entire coastline of Hakata Bay with a defensive wall. Nor were the Mongol troops much motivated to give the attack their all. Cooped up in ships and unable to land except on well-defended beach-heads guarded by fanatical samurai defenders, Khubilai's 'soldiers' were not the fearless Mongol horsemen of old, but largely Chinese conscripts with little interest in risking their lives.

Marco's account of the riches of Japan, which greatly over-exaggerates the wealth of the island nation, may have been based at least in part on Mongol propaganda designed to instil some degree of fighting spirit in such men. There is certainly little grounding in fact for Marco's boasts, and it seems unlikely that Rustichello would have been motivated to lie about a place of which he, and everyone else in Christendom, had never heard. *I will tell you a wonderful thing about the palace of the lord of that island*, he writes. *You must know that he has a great palace, which is entirely roofed with fine gold, just as our churches are roofed with lead, insomuch as it would scarcely be possible to estimate its value. Moreover, all the pavement of the palace, and the floors of its chambers, are entirely of gold, in plates like slabs of stone, a good two fingers thick; and the windows are also of gold, so that altogether the richness of this palace is past all bounds and all belief.[93]*

By a remarkable coincidence, Marco's claims do match a real Japanese place very closely – Kinkakuji, the Temple of the Golden Pavilion, in Kyoto. A retreat in a landscaped garden, with walls and roof covered in gold leaf, Kinkakuji was intended as a 'palace for the ruler' (in fact, the Shogun Ashikaga Yoshimitsu). It cannot, however, have been the place Marco referred to, since it was not built until 1390. The building was destroyed and rebuilt several times, most recently in 1955 after an arson attack.

Despite such promises of booty waiting on the other side of the wall, the sailors and marines of the Mongol invasion fleet had little motivation to face the samurai defenders. Nor does Marco hold back in his descriptions of the Japanese as a truly strange race, whose idols *are so manifold and of such devilish contrivance that it is not proper to speak of them in our book, since they are no fit hearing for Christians*. He also repeats a rumour that may have sprung up among the Mongol forces that the Japanese had a drastic way of dealing with prisoners who were not immediately ransomed by their own forces. If no money arrives to buy a prisoner out of Japanese captivity, writes Marco, his captor *summons all his friends and relations, and they put the prisoner to death, and then they cook him and eat him, and they say there is no meat in the world so good.[94]*

Marco's account of the fight with Japan also includes strange references to supposedly 'invincible' enemies. *As they had refused to surrender, it was ordered that they should all be beheaded. The order was duly carried out. All the prisoners were beheaded except eight men only, whose heads could not be cut off. This happened by virtue of certain stones that they carried on their persons. For each one of them had a stone*

*embedded in his arm, between the flesh and the skin, so that it was not
visible on the surface. This stone possessed a magic property whereby anyone
who had it on his person was proof against steel.*[95]

This tale of Japanese warriors with stones sewn into their flesh
may be couched in mystic terms, but could instead refer to an old
Japanese story that prisoners of war, fearing they might be used
to test new swords, would sometimes swallow rocks before being
led out to execution. The blade
that struck the death blow might
also break on the rocks, giving the
victim some small sense of satisfac-
tion. It is notable also that a strange
custom is rumoured to persist
among modern Japanese criminals,
who sew a pearl under their skin
for each year they spend in jail.
However, the modern variant of the
tale does not refer to their 'arms'
but an altogether more intimate
body part.

Matters were not helped by a
degree of rivalry between Arakhan,
the Mongol general who fell ill *en
route*, and Fan Wenhu, a former

Cannibalism

It might seem strange for Marco to drag
mention of cannibalism into discussion
of Japan, although we might also re-
member that he regarded Cipangu as
just one of several isles of the 'Indies',
and that his later sea voyages would
take him through south-eastern Asian
regions where true cannibalism, or at
least rumours about it, was far more
founded. If he is not repeating a Mongol
war-story, he may simply be confusing
Japan with Sumatra, or another island
where cannibalism was rumoured to be
a part of the way of life.

general of the Southern Song dynasty, who had been granted
a high position in the invasion force, but did not agree with
decisions made by his nominal superior. There appears to have
been some confusion as to who was in charge – Arakhan was ill
enough to have been relieved of his command, but his replacement never arrived, and Arakhan plainly soon recovered enough to
regard himself as restored to active duty. Meanwhile, Fan Wenhu
presumably enjoyed greater respect and loyalty from many of the
troops, most of whom were his Chinese countrymen. He would,

however, be expected to obey the orders of a general who was supposedly too ill to lead an army.

You must know, writes Marco, *that there was much ill-will between those two barons, so that one would do nothing to help the other. And it came to pass that there arose a north wind that blew with great fury, and caused great damage along the coasts of that island, for its harbours were few. It blew so hard that the Great Khan's fleet could not stand against it. And when the chiefs saw that, they came to the conclusion that if the ships remained where they were the whole navy would perish.*[96] In fact, it was less likely to have been the 'chiefs' who were concerned than the Korean sailors, many of whom would have been painfully aware that many of them were sailing in flat-bottomed river boats unsuitable for deep, choppy waters. *But when they had gone about four miles they came to a small island, on which they were driven ashore in spite of all they could do; and a great part of the fleet was wrecked, and a great multitude of the force perished, so that there escaped only some 30,000 men, who took refuge on the island.*[97]

Just as in the first assault, the Mongols were routed by a Divine Wind. Although several thousand escaped, they were marooned on an offshore island, and many were captured and executed by the Japanese victors. Marco's account goes on for some time regarding their adventures on the island – possibly Tsushima, which sits halfway between Japan and Korea, as the Mongols fight with local forces, seize a defensible peninsula, but are then put under siege by pursuing samurai for seven months. The plight of the marooned Mongol forces ends, in Marco's account at least, with their surrender and enslavement. *So when they saw they could hold out no longer, they gave themselves up, on condition that their lives should be spared, but still that they should never quit the island.*[98] Life, for many of them, did not last long past the lifting of the siege; although some were enslaved, most were executed, with a mere three men permitted to leave the island to report their defeat to Khubilai. The ailing general Arakhan was not one of them, although the precise nature of his demise is not recorded – the chronicles of the Yuan dynasty simply note that he 'died in the army'. However, not all the invaders were captured. A number of ships had made it back to China under the command of Fan Wenhu, although the welcome they received was decidedly frosty. Although he was not punished, he never again enjoyed such a high position of authority, and is only mentioned once more in Chinese records, three years later, when he is commanding a garrison of a mere 500 men.[99]

Not even this setback was enough to deter Khubilai. Throughout Marco's early years in China, the Khan fully intended to mount a third expedition against Japan, and only finally gave up on the idea in 1286, when his advisers pressured him to concentrate on more immediate concerns such as the threats posed by Khaidu and Nayan. However, in the intermediate years, Khubilai pushed hard for a national war effort against the Japanese. In 1283, southern Chinese merchants complained at the expense of providing another 500 ships for another doomed attack, while by 1285, Mongol agents were canvassing far inland in Manchuria for assistance building ships, and the Koreans were ordered to stockpile rice ready for an attack. Although Khubilai officially cancelled the operation in 1286, plans for another attack on Japan were clearly a major topic of conversation in the merchant cities – no wonder, if Marco was living in Yangzhou or Hangzhou, he should accord so much importance to Japan. It, and propaganda about it, would have been one of the major news stories of its day, particularly among the occupied Chinese, some of whom may have even felt a sly admiration for a nation that still held out where all China had surrendered.

Over Strange Seas

Although Marco is famous today largely for his sojourn in China, most versions of his book boast of its status as a 'Description of the World'. He also gives brief accounts of other parts of the world as it was known during his time, including tales of the distant wastes of Siberia. One Marco manuscript devotes several pages to the Russian climate, although it is low on anecdotes and high on generalities, as if Marco were simply repeating things he had heard from other travellers. He makes no claim to have visited such regions, although his reports on them bear many elements that suggest he had heard tales about them from Mongol associates. Marco's account of the Arctic tundra calls it *the Land of Darkness, because perpetual darkness reigns there, unlit by sun or moon or star – such darkness as there is in our countries in the early evening ... These people have great quantities of costly furs – sable, whose immense value I have already noted, ermine, ercolin, vair and black fox, and many others.*[100] Marco paints a believable picture of remote Arctic trappers, entering the bounds of daylight to trade their furs – a familiar occurrence all across Asia, from the Black Sea coast to northern China. But Marco seems keen to hurry along in his description of the world – *there is nothing else here worth mentioning*, he claims, apparently eager to get away from hearsay into tales born of his personal experience. The notes on Russia, the Arctic, the Black Sea regions and beyond in Marco's book seem strangely rushed and occur late in the manuscript, as if tacked on grudgingly to help justify the title. As soon as the occasion arises, Marco turns talk of the Black Sea to talk of the conflicts among the Mongols of the area – Hulagu and Barka, a subject he would have known well through many tellings and retellings by his father and uncle.

However, Marco's direct experiences did not stop at China. Towards the end of his time in China, his prologue reports that he *returned from India by a voyage over strange seas and had much to report of his travels.*[101] Notably, the text implies that only his return journey was made by sea – it seems possible, from hints dropped elsewhere in Marco's text that he made another overland journey to the south-west in the late 1280s, in the wake of Mongol invasion forces sent to conquer Burma and Bengal. Marco calls the region Mien, reflecting its modern name of Myanmar – his definition of 'India' encapsulating a far greater area of territory than in modern times.

Battles over south-east Asia continued throughout Marco's time in China, both as the initial conquest, and in order to put down several insurrections. Khubilai regarded the region as an important sector – important enough to leave it under the stewardship of Esen-Temür, his eldest grandson. Champa and Annam, the areas known today as Vietnam and Laos, swiftly dealt with the Mongol threat by swearing fealty and paying tribute, ensuring that they were left alone. The island of Java continued to hold out, benefiting like Japan from the additional difficulties of organising a seaborne assault. But it was in Burma that the Mongols met with their most trying mainland foe, King Narathihapate, who held out against Mongol incursions throughout the 1280s. Although he was ultimately defeated, and forced to pay a ransom to clear Mongol occupiers from his own capital, Narathihapate's resistance drew Marco to leave a detailed account of some of his finest moments.

And when the king's army had arrived in the plain, and was within a mile of the enemy, he caused all the castles that were on the elephants to be ordered for battle, and the fighting men to take up their posts on them, and he arrayed his horse and his foot with all skill, like a wise king as he was. And when he had completed all his arrangements, he began to advance to engage the enemy.[102]

Marco's account, despite his Mongol sympathies, shows an uncanny degree of respect for the Burmese ruler, and an appreciation of fear and valour on both sides that may suggest his physical presence at the battle he describes. Certainly, his account of the use of elephants in combat is not an idle fantasy, but full of first-person observations, such as the terror the massive creatures struck into the Mongol horses. The Mongols were obliged to tether their mounts in the forest and go after the elephants with bows and arrows. *Understand that when the elephants felt the smart of those arrows that pelted them like rain, they turned tail and fled, and nothing on earth would have induced them to turn and face the Tartars. So off they sped with such a noise and uproar that you would have thought the world was coming to an end. And then too they plunged into the wood and rushed this way and that, dashing the castles against the trees, bursting their harness and smashing and destroying everything that was on them.*[103]

As Marco notes himself, the victory in Burma also led to the capture of 200 war-elephants, which were brought back to China and entered Khubilai's own military service. But even if he had been present at their capture, he did not accompany them back across the mountains into China. His own route seems to have taken him downriver back towards the sea, where he somehow found his way onboard a ship heading back towards China.

For many centuries, particularly during the 'Dark Ages', shipping on the Indian Ocean and in the China Seas was largely in the hands of Arab merchants. But during the Song dynasty that preceded the Mongol conquest, the Chinese had become far more pro-active in their foreign trade. Ships did not merely use the safe, calm waters of the Grand Canal to move goods from south to north China, but sailed along the coast, too. In the south, sailors put forth from the great ports of Quanzhou and Fuzhou and sailed across the Indian Ocean, as far as the Persian Gulf and the east coast of Africa.

This long-distance trade continued under Mongol rule, and stayed largely in Chinese hands – the horse-riding Mongols preferring to steer clear of the sea wherever possible, particularly in the wake of marine disasters like the attempted invasion of Japan. Contemporary European shipping, which either hugged the Atlantic coasts or sailed the relatively calm waters of the Mediterranean, was usually far smaller than the ocean-going vessels of Chinese merchants, and Marco's description of the sea-going giants would have been regarded with some cynicism among many European readers. *The crew needed to man a ship ranges from 150 to 300 according to her size*, he writes. *They carry a much bigger cargo than ours.*[105] The vessel on which Marco implies he sailed had a single deck, and a superstructure

Pygmies

Marco mentions surprisingly few medieval 'marvels'. In fact, he is often keener to dispel superstitions and rumours: *when people bring home pygmies which they allege to come from India, it is all a lie and a cheat ... for there is ... a kind of monkey* [possibly an orang utan or proboscis monkey] *which is very small and has a face just like a man's. They take these and pluck out all the hair except the hair of the beard ... and then they dry them and stuff them and daub them with saffron ... until they look like men.*[104]

of some 60 cabins, *each of which can comfortably accommodate one merchant*. It had four fixed masts, and two auxiliary masts that could be raised where necessary. Marco states that hulls were made initially of double rows of spruce or fir planking, caulked with a lime and hemp paste pounded together *with the oil of a tree*. Here he is probably referring to Tong oil – the pressed juices of the fruits of trees of the genus *Aleurites fordii* or *Aleurites montana*. As late as the 20th century, Chinese sailors were still reported as mixing Tong oil with lime and bamboo shavings to make a waterproof paste.

Marco reports that each of the most massive ships is part of a small flotilla of tender craft – several somewhat smaller craft that two the larger vessels both under oars and sails. Each of the ships also carries several small boats for landing and supplies, with the largest mounting up to ten boats on its sides.

Marco also reports a bizarre ritual undertaken before sailing, in which a hapless member of the crew would be tied to a large kite – Marco uses the term 'hurdle' in his own account, since kites appear to have been unknown in the West until the 14th century, and his account may have been the first time that such a device was mentioned in a European language. *The seamen will take a hurdle – that is, a frame of wickerwork – and to every corner and side of it they will attach a rope ... Next they will find someone who is drunk – for no one in his right sense would expose himself to so much risk – and lash him to the hurdle. This they do when it is blowing a gale. Then they set the hurdle upright in the teeth of the wind and the wind lifts it and carries it aloft, while the men hold it by hanging onto the cable.*[106] Marco places enough credence and importance on the ritual that it could make or break a ship's fortunes for the year. If the kite went straight up in the air in strong winds, local merchants would regard it as a favourable omen, and queue up for the opportunity to sail with the ship. If it failed to rise at all, it was considered to be a portent of doom, and interest in booking passage on such a ship would be so low that it would probably not sail at all that year.

Considering that Marco would have been largely in the company of Chinese rather than Mongols or Persians, and that consequently his ability to hold conversations would have been limited, was Marco the gullible passenger being taken in by a tall tale from an old sea-dog? Kites had been in use in China for many centuries, and there are many accounts of man-sized versions being used in military (and presumably naval) reconnaissance over the years, but the stunt as performed by the drunken kite-rider seems remarkably dangerous. Nor would Marco have seen it in south-east Asia, since his description implies that it was done in Chinese waters at the outward leg of a journey to foreign climes, not on the homeward journey. Although Marco may be telling the truth (he has, after all, been proved right on so many other 'unlikely' claims in his text), it seems possible that if the ritual he describes existed at all, it may have been reserved for missions of deep significance and importance, such as the final journey that he took out of China on imperial business, discussed in a later chapter.

Marco's European readers would have been shocked and appalled to hear of his southernmost wanderings, when his ship followed the coast of Sumatra. *But let me premise one marvellous thing, and that is the fact that this island lies so far to the south that the North Star, little or much, is never seen.*[107] To medieval readers unsure of the precise geography or indeed physics of the world, the very idea would have suggested that Marco Polo might be approaching the ends of the Earth, so far to the south that the northern sky was no longer visible. His brief mention of the phenomenon represented the final corner of his text's journey, in the sense that he had now dealt with the arctic north, the tropical south, and the furthest conceivable point east (Japan). The west, as the home of both Marco and his readers, was included by default; Marco's book now encapsulated all parts of the known world.

His return journey took him to the southeast Chinese city of Quanzhou, *which is the port for all the ships that arrive from India laden with costly wares and precious stones of great price and big pearls of fine quality ... From this city and its port goods are exported to the whole {of China}.*[108] Shielded from the rest of China by a wall of mountains, the coves and bays of southwest China made travel between coastal settlements often easier by ship than by land. It was only natural that the area would become the centre of Chinese trade, particularly since it was close to Taiwan, and from there to the Ryukyu island chain that led up to Japan. The men of the region were renowned sailors, and Marco reports that their abilities made the area a nexus of trade. At many points through Chinese history, the region was regarded as fractious and difficult to govern, although it does not seem to have presented much of a problem for the Mongols, who simply took a 10 per cent cut of all trade. The sailors themselves often had little to do with their cargoes, instead renting their ships out to merchants, who would then pay between 30 and 44 per cent of their profits to the crew. *So that, what with freight and the imperial tithe*, writes Marco, *the merchants pay half the value of what they import. And yet from the half that falls to their share they make such a profit that they ask nothing better than to return with another cargo. So you may readily believe that this city's contribution to the Great Khan's treasury is no small one.*[109]

Quanzhou Customs

Not everyone was as pleased as Marco with the treatment of merchants in Quanzhou. A generation later, Abu Abdullah Muhammad ibn Battuta also visited Quanzhou, and noted: 'They order the ship's master to dictate to them a manifest of all the merchandise in it, whether small or great. Then everyone disembarks and the customs officials sit to inspect what they have with them. If they come upon any article that has been concealed from them the junk and whatever is in it is forfeit to the treasury. This is a kind of extortion I have seen in no country, whether infidel or Muslim, except in China.'[110]

Marco was very taken with Quanzhou, which he referred to by its Arabic name, Zaiton ('olives'). This in turn was taken from the genus of the many groves of trees that turned wide city lanes into dappled avenues. The trees had been planted by a governor during the Song dynasty, and endured for long after Marco's visit. The city boasted a community of Arab and Persian merchants, and it would seem that Marco spent his time in their company. He not only refers to the city by its Arab name, but notes: *The inhabitants of this city have their own distinctive speech* – a subtle complaint that the local Hokkien dialect is incomprehensible to anyone speaking standard Mandarin, particularly one such as Marco, whose Chinese seems to have been rudimentary at best.[111]

Despite such apparent difficulties in communication, Marco

took to Quanzhou with all the enthusiasm of a traveller who had endured long months of deprivation on the road and aboard ship. His comments on the city are matched only by his earlier words of praise for the fleshpots of Hangzhou. *It is a delightful place*, he writes, *amply supplied with all that the human body requires; and the inhabitants are peaceable folk, fond of leisure and easy living.*[112]

A Passage to India

Khubilai Khan's beloved wife Chabi passed away in 1281, and notably became the only one of the Khan's wives to get her own memorial tablet in the ancestral temple. The extent of Chabi's contribution to Khubilai's administration only became clear in her absence. A relative, Nambi, became Khubilai's new chief wife, and soon a prime messenger between the despondent Khan and his ministers. It was suspected the Nambi began issuing edicts in Khubilai's name, although this may simply be an attempt by court chroniclers to blame her for Khubilai's mistakes in later years. Chabi's eldest son by Khubilai, Jenjin, also died in 1285.

By the 1290s, Khubilai was no longer the young, strong conqueror who had carried the banners of Genghis Khan to the corners of Asia. In China, he was still the Son of Heaven, but he was the Great Khan in name only in many parts of Asia. In the western reaches of his realm, local Mongol rulers paid only lip-service to his suzerainty, or, in the case of Khaidu, openly opposed it. Their disloyalty caused much of the Mongol conquest to stumble – in the distant Holy Land, the Muslims gained ground once more. On the borders of China, Japan remained defiant, and Khubilai did little about it.

He had other things on his mind. To the north of Beijing, his Chinese engineers dug the massive hollow that would become Kunming Lake, a reservoir to slake the thirst of the growing population of Khanbalikh. But Khubilai's public works were of less importance to him than his private celebrations. Disconsolate at the deaths of his favourite wife and son during the 1280s, Khubilai flung himself into palace banquets and festivities. Already a portly old man, he grew morbidly obese on meaty Mongol dishes, and succumbed to alcoholism – an affliction that was the ruin of many a Mongol leader. Meanwhile, the Polo family members seem to have developed a degree of concern for what would happen to them and other *semuren* after Khubilai's impending death. *They applied to him several times for leave to go, presenting their request with great respect, but he {was so fond of} them, and liked to much to have them about him, that nothing on earth would persuade him to let them go.*[113]

It is not entirely clear why the Polos were so keen to get out of China. There were wars in Inner Asia that cut off the Silk Road, but there had been wars somewhere in the Khan's realm throughout their time in China. The news may have reached them of the death of Marco's uncle 'Marco the Elder', and neither Niccolo nor Maffeo would have been getting any younger. Homesickness alone is probably enough of an excuse, particularly if tales of foreign travel had lost their lustre and, for whatever reason, a *semuren*'s life was no longer as glamorous and rewarding as it had once been.

Arghun (c.1258–91)

The grandson of Hulagu and son of Abaqa, Arghun Khan was the ruler of the Mongol Ilkhanate region, roughly equivalent to modern Iran, Afghanistan, Azerbaijan and parts of Pakistan. A Buddhist ruler who despised Muslims, Arghun had made several unsuccessful attempts to join forces with the Christian west against Islam, and had been one of the patrons of the Nestorian monk Rabban Sauma.

An unexpected opportunity arose in Persia, where death claimed Queen Bulagan, the wife of Khubilai's great-nephew Arghun (and of his predecessor, Abaqa). One of the queen's dying stipulations had been that only a woman of her own lineage could replace her. Three emissaries duly fought their way across Asia on horseback to report this to Khubilai Khan. *The Khan received them with all honour and hospitality, and then sent for a lady whose name was Kokachin, who was of the family of the deceased Queen Bulagan. She was a maiden of 17, a very beautiful and charming person, and on her arrival at court she was presented to the three Barons ... They declared that the Lady pleased them well.*[114] However, owing to insurrections in Asia, there was now no safe land route back to Persia. The three emissaries and their royal ward seemed doomed to stay for a while in China, until they heard of Marco's recent return to China by sea. Despite traditional Mongol qualms about taking to the water, they were assured by Marco's reports that marine travel was perfectly safe.

And the three Barons, having seen that Messer Niccolo, Messer Maffeo and Messer Marco were not only Latins, but men of marvellous good sense withal, took thought among themselves to get the three to travel with them, their intention being to return to their country by sea, on account on the great fatigue of that long land journey for a lady. And the ambassadors were the more desirous to have their company, as being aware that those three had great knowledge and experience of the Indian Sea and the countries by which they would have to pass ... So they went to the Great Khan and begged as a favour that he would send the three Latins with them ... The Lord, having great regard that I have mentioned for those three Latins, was very loath to do so, and his countenance showed great dissatisfaction. But at last he did give them permission to depart, enjoining them to accompany the three Barons and the Lady.[115]

The Polos, it seems, promised that they would return to China once their mission was complete, although all the parties understood it would be a long haul. Although unmentioned here, another part of Marco's narrative adds that Khubilai *entrusted to their care not only the Princess Kokachin, but also the daughter of the King of {China}.*[116] However, while Marco's book frames the whole thing as an almost chivalric undertaking – chaperoning a pretty young princess, possibly with her royal lady-in-waiting, to her distant bridegroom – it is not difficult to sense that Marco may have been economical with the truth. He admits that there was a

Gary Cooper as Marco Polo and Sigrid Gurie as Princess Kokachin in the 1938 film *The Adventures of Marco Polo.*

political dimension, since Khubilai *charged them also with messages to the King of France, the King of England, the King of Spain and the other kings of Christendom.* However, Marco's party may have been part of another mission altogether, and journeyed at least part of the way in the company of a Mongol invasion fleet.

When the Polos set out, Khubilai presented them with a

paizi, or a Mongol passport. These gold or silver tablets had long been used in nomad-influenced realms as symbols of the Khan's authority – originally they had been used as legal waivers to permit imperial messengers to seize fresh horses wherever required. During Khubilai's reign, they had a more general use, and bore an inscription proclaiming: 'By the strength of the Great God and of the great grace which he hath accorded to our Emperor, may the name of the Khan be blessed; and let all such as will not obey him be slain and be destroyed.'[117] Such an item was, in theory, enough to guarantee Marco's safety in the Mongol realm, but would not have been much use on the seaborne part of his travels.

His journey on the Indian Ocean was not the voyage of a single ship, but that of *a great company of people, and with all necessaries provided for two years by the Emperor.*[118] Marco's text also contradicts itself as to the exact route. His Prologue claims that he sailed via Java, as a member of a mission of 600 members, subsumed within a far larger company, the precise nature of which is never disclosed. Much later in his text, when he alludes to the same mission, he mentions stopping off in Sumatra, waiting for seasonal winds to shift so that his convoy could continue its journey.[119] *This is how we spent our five months. We disembarked from our ships and for fear of these nasty and brutish folk {the Sumatrans} who kill men for food we dug a big trench around our encampment, extending down to the shore of the harbour at either end. On the embankment of the trench we built five wooden towers or forts; and within these fortifications we lived for five months.*[120]

It is a strangely militaristic account of what is otherwise implied to be a simple diplomatic or trading mission. The precise date of Marco's five-month sojourn is not specified – Marco passed through the region at least twice, once heading towards China after a *semuren* mission, and once again heading back towards Europe. But far from simply waiting for the weather, Marco may have been in the company of a Mongol invasion force that set sail from Quanzhou in 1292. Its target was Java, whose king Kertanagara had defied Mongol ambassadors in 1289. Marco's text clearly differentiates between Sumatra and Java, but fighting in the campaign against Kertanagara spread right across Indochina, with skirmishes in what is now Vietnam and Malaya. It is not all that difficult to believe that Marco's embassy to the west made at least part of its journey as part of a much larger fleet on an altogether more martial mission.

One of the rarer Marco texts mentions that there *were about 2,000 people who were in his company* – could this be a copyist's error for the 20,000 soldiers who were known to have gone on the 1292 Javan invasion?[121] The records of the Yuan dynasty make it clear that the invasion fleet was of a size comparable to that which had attacked Japan – boasting a thousand ships, several tonnes of silver to buy provisions, and a year's worth of grain for immediate consumption. Compare this to the *provisions for two years* that Marco's Prologue claims he was given by Khubilai.

Although Marco never returned to the Far East, he felt himself to be enough of an expert on the subject of Java to comment *the great Khan has never been able to conquer it* – had he not been with the Java task force, he would surely have left China believing that the Mongol

Dog Faces?

In the area of the Andaman islands, Marco made a comment about the non-Aryan, non-Semitic features of the local people that has been misinterpreted by some of his later readers. *You may take it for a fact that all the men of this island have heads like dogs, and teeth and eyes like dogs.*[123] To a medieval readership raised on 'marvels' like Cyclopes and giants, this was taken literally, as if the Andaman islands were populated by creatures that resembled the Egyptian god Anubis.

fleet stood a good chance of success.[122] But whether the Polos and Princess Kokachin spent the first year of their mission sailing with the invasion fleet or not, their own group had struck out alone for India by 1293.

En route to India, Marco reported on the land of Basman, a place boasting wild elephants and *plenty of unicorns, which are very nearly as big. They have hair like that of a buffalo, feet like those of an elephant's, and a horn in the middle of the forehead, which is black and very thick. They do no mischief, however, with the horn, but with the tongue alone, for this is covered all over with long and strong prickles and when savage with anyone they crush him under their knees and then rasp him with their tongue.*[124] The creature Marco describes is widely believed to be based on highly garbled references to a rhinoceros.

From Sumatra, Marco's ships left coastal waters and sailed straight for the Andaman and Nicobar islands, where rough waters and deceptive currents threatened to maroon him. However, the fleet made it through, setting out once more across open seas for India itself, and making landfall at Sri Lanka, where Marco reacted with his customary elation at a completed journey, and rated it *undoubtedly the finest island of its size in all the world.*[125] He was less taken with Sri Lanka's inhabitants, who appeared reluctant to part with some of the precious gems that could be found on the island. He calls them *paltry and mean-spirited creatures* and soon notes that *there is nothing else here worth mentioning*.

A few dozen pages later, he changes his mind, and returns abruptly to the subject of the island, after several religious anecdotes from India remind him that he did indeed see something of great interest in Sri Lanka. As Marco got closer to Europe, he began to pay greater attention to religious matters in his narrative, seemingly realising that readers in Christendom would be far more interested in pious reportage than in notes on strange animals and bizarre herbs.

Inland from the Sri Lankan coast lies Sri Pada (Sanskrit: 'the sacred footprint'), a cone-shaped mountain rising 2,243 metres (7,360 feet) above sea level. Other local names for it reflect its sacred status – the Jewelled Hill, the Climb to Heaven or even Wanton with Butterflies, since so many insects are lured in a one-way journey up its slopes, only to die in their thousands at the peak. The peak, which can only be reached after a long and difficult climb, was already a site of pilgrimage in Marco's day. *For many iron chains have been hung on the side of the mountain, so arranged that by their means a man can climb to the top.*[126] Near the summit, a strange depression in the rock resembles a human left footprint, which local tradition claimed was that of the god Shiva. Muslim tradition held that it was actually that of Adam, who had either stepped onto the mountain as he descended from heaven after Creation, or that he was relocated to Sri Lanka after his exile from Eden, and could stand on the very top of the mountain in order to get his head close enough to heaven to hear the voices of angels.

Tempting though it must have been for Marco to leave his comments at that, and to describe 'Adam's Peak' as it is also known as a marvel of Christian interest, he notes with a stern critical eye that *we do not believe that Adam is in this place, since our Scripture of the Holy Church declares that he is in another part of the world* – a puzzling reliance on European tradition when one considers his willingness to overturn earlier legends such as those of the Three Magi.[127] Instead, Marco bravely notes that still another religion has a claim on Sri Pada. *The Saracens say that it is Adam's grave, but the idolaters call it the monument of Sakaymuni Burkhan* [Buddha].[128]

Marco's account of the life of Buddha is outstandingly accurate, and presumably draws not only on many years in Mongol China in the company of Buddhists, but his personal presence in Khanba-likh at which Buddhist relics were presented to Khubilai. He notes, perhaps taking his cue from one of Khubilai's comments, that Buddha was the first man in whose name idols were made, and goes on to recount many elements of the life story of Buddha – his birth into a rich and royal family, his early life in careful and luxurious seclusion, and his sudden, shocking encounter with death and old age. *When the king's son had thus learned about the dead man and the aged man, he turned back to his palace and said to himself*

*that he would abide no longer in this evil world, but would go in search
of Him Who dieth not, and Who had created him ... {Fleeing his palace,
he} betook himself to certain lofty and pathless mountains. And there he
did abide, leading a life of great hardship and sanctity, and keep great
abstinence, just as if he had been a Christian. Indeed, if he had but been
so, he would have been a great saint of
Our Lord Jesus Christ.*[129]

Gautama Siddhartha
(c.563–c.483 BC)

The historical Buddha was born in what
is now Nepal, the son of King Suddho-
dana. Following predictions at his birth
that he would grow to be a great king
or a great holy man, he was raised in seclusion, in the hope that he would not
witness human suffering. This scheme
ultimately backfired, and, traumatised
by the sight of death and old age, the
prince became a wandering monk. He
achieved 'enlightenment' aged 35, and
became the founder of the religious tradition that bears his name. Although
widely known as *Buddha* (Sanskrit: 'En-
lightened'), he was known to Marco as
Burkhan (Mongol: 'Divine').

Marco's knowledge of the story
of the Buddha and its relation-
ship to Sri Pada is not necessarily
based on his personal experience.
In 1284, when Marco was serving
as a *semuren* in China, Khublai sent
an embassy to India to purchase the
relics of Buddha on the mountain –
the shrine at its summit supposedly
containing two of Buddha's teeth,
some of his hair, and his magical
bowl. Supposedly, the mission was
a success; at least the Khan's ambassadors were sure to bring back
artefacts matching the description,
and were received back in Khanbalikh with great ceremony. Khubilai
even reported, in one of his careful

appeasements of multicultural traditions, that he had privately
filled the bowl with food enough for one, and that it had fed five,
just as legend dictated.[130]

Marco also found himself to be less than welcome in some
Indian places – if not openly despised, then certainly patronised.
Most of the people here abstain from drinking wine, he notes, alcohol
being a recurring subject in many places in his book. *They will
not admit as a witness or a guarantor either a wine-drinker or one who*

sails on the sea – a second category in which Marco would have been most assuredly placed, considering his means of transport. *For they say that a man who goes to sea must be a man in despair. On the other hand you should know that they do not regard any form of sexual indulgence as a sin.*[131] Considering Marco's past comments on sexual indulgence around the world, it would seem that he had finally found some common ground with the Indians.

Although Marco has little more to say about his adventures with Indian women, he did find the time to ogle, and possible grope a few temple dancers during his visit, and noted the sensual nature of some Indian religious statues. *So these maidens go to the monastery … and there, completely naked, except that they cover their private parts, they sing before the god and goddess … And the people say that {the god} often dallies with {the goddess} and they have sexual intercourse together; but when they are estranged … these maidens come to placate them. When they are there, they devote themselves to singing, dancing, leaping, tumbling, and every sort of exercise designed to amuse … and then the maiden … will lift her leg higher than her neck and perform a pirouette for the delectation of the god and goddess.*[132]

Rani Rudramma Devi
(c.1247–c.1295)

The only child of King Ganapathideva, who ruled a small state on the Deccan plateau, Rudramma was ceremonially raised as a boy, succeeding to her father's throne at the age of 14. Ruling for over 30 years, Rudramma's upbringing left her uninterested in most 'feminine' pursuits, although she did enjoy some temple dances, and added a series of dance moves to her army's exercise routine. The date of her death, and Marco's apparent ignorance of it, helps date his arrival in and departure from India to sometime around 1293/4.

Marco was quite taken with the temple girls, and noted with great interest their pert, firm bosoms and their taut, tight flesh – *for a penny they will allow a man to pinch them as hard as he can*, he adds, without daring to suggest that he had the right change.

He also wrote reports of convicted criminals dedicating their lives to an idol before they committed ritual suicide, and also the phenomenon of self-immolation, or *sati*, by widows. *When a man is dead and his body is being cremated, his wife flings herself into the same fire and lets herself be burnt with her husband. The ladies who do this are highly praised by all. And I assure you that there are many who do as I have told you.*[133]

Marco was clearly quite stunned by this tradition, and soon found noble Indian widows wherever her looked. On the east coast of India, Marco heard tales of a kingdom to the north, *ruled by a queen, who is a very wise woman*, but mistakenly assumed that she was a widow. *I can tell you that throughout her forty years' reign* (Marco confuses the queen's age with her term of office), *she has governed her kingdom well with a high standard of justice and equity, as her husband did before.*

Along the coast of India proper, Marco was most impressed by the weather. *The climate is amazingly hot, which explains why they go naked … If it were not for the rain … which freshens the air, the heat would be so oppressive that no one could stand it.*[134] He found himself in a land of strange idols and bizarre behaviours, and reported with some accuracy on the presence of pearl divers off the coast, the reverence of the Indians for cows, and the treatment of members of the untouchable caste. *When {Hindus} have a mind to eat the flesh of a sheep or of any beast or bird, they employ a Saracen or some other who is not of their religion or rule to kill it for them.*[135]

As Marco rounded the tip of India and sailed north along the subcontinent's western coast, he continued to see and report on marvellous things, beasts and customs but also seemed aware that he was leaving 'strange seas' behind and entering a realm that had much more in common with his own homeland. *I will tell you plainly of the customs and products of this country*, he says, *and you will be able to understand them better, because we are now approaching more civilized places.*[136]

The Return Home

Despite the obvious westward drive of Marco's itinerary, his text is still confused, even in the deceptive simplicity of a journey up along the Indian coast and then to Persia. As seen above in his sudden brainstorm regarding sites of interest in Sri Lanka, he was still apt to interpolate anecdotes that did not necessarily belong in a particular place in the text. This would become increasingly prevalent as the Polo family entered the Middle East, affording Marco with the opportunity to mention incidents from the *outward* journey that he may have forgotten the first time. Possibly, it may also have given Rustichello a freer rein to include his own stories, since the Polos' travels now drew them inexorably towards the Holy Land, and places of which Marco's co-author also had direct experience and tall tales to tell.

Even the local idols became more familiar to Marco. Along the Malabar coast of India, he found a shrine to St. Thomas, *a place of great pilgrimage for Saracens and Christians ... You must know that the Christians who go there on pilgrimage take some of the earth from the place where the saintly body died and carry it back to their own country. Then, when anyone falls sick ... they give him a little of this earth to drink. And no sooner has he done it than he is cured.*[137] One manuscript of Marco's book goes even further, stating that Marco himself scooped up some of the miraculous earth, and carried it with him back to his homeland.

A devoted disciple of Jesus, who once offered to lay down his life at Jesus' side, the chief source for St. Thomas is the *Gospel of St. John*, which reports his professed willingness to die at the side of Jesus, and his bewilderment at the Last Supper when Jesus promises to return from the grave. Biblically, he is famous as the 'doubting Thomas' who initially refused to believe in the Resurrection. Early Christian legends held that Thomas became an evangelist in the east, converting many Syrians to Christianity, before being killed while preaching in Madras, India around AD 53. This later story may have been introduced by Syrian refugees in India, many of whom moved there in the 9th century, and became known as Malabar Christians, or St. Thomas Christians.

The tradition of St. Thomas as a protector of the region's Christians was strong at the time that Marco arrived. A story alleged to have happened a few years earlier (he places it in 1288) suggests that a local ruler angered the spirit of St. Thomas by using buildings of the saint's shrine as silos for rice. *On the night after he had filled them Messer St Thomas the Apostle appeared to him with a fork in his hand and held it to the baron's throat, saying: 'Either you will empty my houses forthwith, or if you do not you must needs die an evil death.'*[138]

As the apostle widely believed to have travelled to Africa and the Indies, St. Thomas crops up often in Marco's narrative of his journey home, although some of the references are not in the Toledo manuscript, implying that they were added by misguided copyists in later, less reliable editions. After such detailed and often verifiable descriptions of China earlier in his book, his chapter on the Indian Ocean and Africa is riddled with errors. However, this is perhaps only to be expected – while he makes many mistakes in his comments on the region, he also makes no claim of having been there himself. Much of what Marco has to say about the area seems instead based on things he heard from fellow travellers on his ship, or could even be enthusiastic interpolations from Rustichello.

Marco describes many African creatures with some accuracy – lynxes and leopards, and a detailed account of the giraffe: *You must know that the giraffe is short in the body ... but the front legs and the neck are so long that the head is fully three paces above the ground.*[139] However, other 'observations' seem to owe more to tales from the *Arabian Nights*. We might imagine Marco listening with rapt interest to his Muslim shipmates as they tell him tales of elephants, which he would know to be true, lions, which he would similarly have seen for himself, and then the new story of something that he calls a 'gryphon bird'. Actual eyewitnesses, so Marco claimed, had told him that it was *all the world like an eagle, but one indeed of enormous size ... And it is so strong that it will seize an elephant in its talons and carry him high into the air and drop him so that he is smashed to pieces; having so killed him the bird ... swoops down on him and eats him at leisure.*[140]

Other notes must surely have even seemed unlikely to him even as he wrote them down. An aside, seemingly added as an afterthought long after he had finished talking about elephants, claims that they copulated in the missionary position, for which they needed to find a hollow in the ground so that the female elephant was correctly situated.

Rocs

Legends of the *rukh* ('roc') had circulated in the Arab world since the 8th century, and may have been based in part on the Aepyornis, an extinct half-tonne ostrich-like bird native to Madagascar, whose remains may have been believed to be those of a chick of an even larger creature. The head of a fully-grown Aepyornis would have been ten feet (three metres) off the ground, making Marco's estimate that such a 'chick' could produce an eagle-like bird with a wingspan of 30 paces not seem so illogical. The legend of the roc gained added momentum after its appearance in the *Arabian Nights*, when one was said to have attacked Sinbad's ship.

When it comes to the denizens of Africa, Marco's comments reflect the prejudices of his day, not merely of his Muslim companions, but of Europeans in general. His notes on Zanzibar (Arabic: *Zanj-i-bar*, 'Coast of the Blacks') seem to draw more on personal observation of black sailors or slaves on his ship. *They are both tall and stout, but not tall in proportion to their stoutness, for if they were, being so stout and brawny, they would be absolutely like giants; and they are so strong that they will carry for four men and eat for five. They are all black, and go stark naked, with only a little covering for decency. Their hair is as black as pepper, and so frizzly that even with water you can scarcely straighten it. And their mouths are so large, their noses so turned up, their lips so thick, their eyes so big and bloodshot, that they look like ... devils; they are in fact so hideously ugly that the world has nothing to show more horrible.*[141]

Nor does Marco, the long-time connoisseur of female beauty, have much positive to say about African women. *The women of this island are the ugliest in the world, with their great mouths and big eyes and thick noses; their breasts too are four times bigger than those of any other women; a very disgusting sight.*[142]

When it comes to matters of actual African geography, Marco's knowledge seems largely limited to Muslim Africa. He comments approvingly that the king of Ethiopia is a Christian, ruling over provinces of mixed Christian and Muslim populations, but much of what he sees seems to be through Arab eyes. He is less impressed with Aden, the great port, noting *that it is the port to which all the ships from India come with their merchandise*, and on the relatively short and easy route that Indian goods need to take to reach Alexandria.

By the time he is writing of Aden, Marco has other things on his mind. His own ship was not bound for there, but for Hormuz, that port on the entrance to the Persian Gulf where he had once pronounced the ships unseaworthy, unaware that he would one day be arriving there in one such ship, after a voyage of many months.

When the Polos finally reached Persia, their company was but a fraction of its former glory. Through natural attrition, the division of parties on other missions, or, as Marco's Prologue boldly states, a remarkable number of deaths, the original party of 600 (or 2,000, or 20,000) was now reduced to just 18. Versions of Marco's book also disagree about their female companions – some suggest that only the Princess Kokachin survived, others that 98 other women made it – a considerable advance on other claims that Kokachin had been unaccompanied, or had a single attendant with her.

However many members there were now surviving in their company, they were still obliged to ride across Persia towards the domain of Arghun, the Mongol vassal who had, they presumed, been patiently waiting for his new bride somewhere near Tabriz. Marco's text becomes confusing again at this point, but for a different reason. Since he was now briefly retracing the steps of his outward journey, he made no further comment on his route – we are thus obliged to piece together his movements of the next nine months or so by returning to his earlier chapters, and sifting through his earlier notes.

Their troubles were still not over. After a journey that had taken the better part of two years, the travellers arrived at their destination only to discover that Arghun, Princess Kokachin's intended husband, was dead – *he died of an illness, though rumour has it that he was poisoned.*[143] Arghun's son, Ghazan, was holding out with an army on the east shore of the Caspian Sea up near the 'Dry Tree', but most of Arghun's domain was in the hands of his brother, Kaikhatu (Geikhatu).

The Dry Tree

On the northern borders of Persia, writes Marco, *there is an immense plain … in which stands the Solitary Tree, which the Christians call the Dry Tree … It is of great size and girth. Its leaves are green on one side, white on the other. It produces husks like chestnut husks, but there is nothing in them.*[144] The tree was supposedly the site of an ancient battle between Alexander the Great and the fugitive Darius III, in the aftermath of the historical battle of Gaugamela.

The early chapters of Marco's book disagree with the later chapters about what happened next. In Marco's account of conflicts between Mongol vassals, he explicitly states that *Kaikhatu continued to rule and all obeyed him except such as were with Ghazan. Kaikhatu took the wife of Arghun for his own, and was always dallying with women, for he was a great lecher. He held the throne for {four} years, and at the end of those two years he died; for you must know that he was poisoned.*[145]

The reference to 'the wife of Arghun' could refer to a number of women, and might even have been Princess Kokachin herself – technically Arghun could not have 'married' anyone else, since that was the whole reason for Kokachin's journey in the first place.

Alaodin

Marco's description of the region also includes a digression about someone he calls Alaodin, the Sheikh of the Mountain, a local ruler who set up a pleasure garden in a hidden valley, and then claim to drugged new recruits that they had visited the paradise promised to the faithful in the Koran. *{F}illed with a great longing to go to this paradise … they longed for death*, thereby allowing their master to send them on suicide missions.[147] Marco appears to be describing the fanatical sect known as the 'Assassins', and their leader Hasan-i-Sabbah (c.1034–1124).

However, it seems more likely that the widows Kaikhatu stole were the widows Bulugan (no relation to the other Bulugan) and Uruk.[146] Marco also states that he left Tabriz while Kaikhatu was still alive, after a stay of nine months. However, he also says that Kaikhatu had no interest in Kokachin, and ordered that the Polos should escort her to Ghazan, the man who would have been her stepson, had her betrothed survived. *And so they did*, says Marco's Prologue tersely.

Those paltry four words are the only evidence Marco offers that he and his companions did not simply abandon Kokachin in the clutches of the usurper. Marco notes that, by the time he sat down to write his book, Kaikhatu had died and his successor, Baidu, had been overthrown by the vengeful prince Ghazan, who had converted from Buddhism to Islam in the interim. *Both Ghazan, who is now the reigning prince, and the Queen Kokachin his wife, have such a regard for the Envoys that there is nothing they would not do for them. And when the three Ambassadors took leave of that Lady to return to their own country, she wept for sorrow at the parting.*[148]

Although he did not write his history until years after Marco left Persia, the chronicler Rashid al-Din (1247–1317) may have been a source for many of Marco's Middle Eastern anecdotes. Rashid was a Jewish convert to Islam who first appears in Muslim records as a physician to Abaqa Khan. He was presumably dismissed at the death of his master, and was hence not implicated in the poison scandal around the death of Arghun. Reinstated as a steward to Kaikhatu, he probably met the Polos during their sojourn at Kaikhatu's court. He later became deputy vizier to Ghazan. In the early decade of the 1300s, he was commissioned by Ghazan to write a chronicle of Mongol history, which grew into the multi-volume *Jami al-Tawarikh*, the largest work of medieval history. However, his own account of the chaos of Kaikhatu's reign is just as sparse as Marco's.

Marco presents a happy ending, with Ghazan regaining his birthright and a wife of royal lineage, although the role of the Polos in this remains unclear. They plainly arrived during the reign of the usurper Kaikhatu, who Marco describes as *not a lawful ruler*.[149] Kaikhatu not only seized the throne, but did so at a time of extreme financial crisis in his kingdom. He tried to alleviate the problem by introducing the concept of paper money from China, which plunged the country into chaos. But it was Kaikhatu who presented the Polos with new golden 'passport' tablets that permitted them to travel through his war-torn realm – they may not have liked him, and they may have realised that he had stolen his throne, but they still enjoyed his hospitality. *Throughout the country they received ample and excellent supplies of everything needful; and many a time, indeed, as I may tell you, they were furnished with 200 horsemen, more or less, to escort them on their way in safety.*[150]

There is, therefore, a certain irony in what happened next. Having safely travelled all the way from southeast China, through several war zones and across many foreign lands, Marco and his elders completed the next leg of their homeward journey as they

Marco Polo being denied entrance to the Polo house in Venice, having not been recognized by his family after an absence of 20 years.

had begun it, bearing golden tablets that granted them the full protection of the Great Khan throughout the world, regardless of the squabbles of petty kinglets. Despite a state of civil war in Kaikhatu's region, the Polos travelled there as safely as if they had been in Khanbalikh itself, finally leaving the realm of the Mongols and Muslims behind, and reaching Trebizond on the shores of the Black Sea. After 20 years away, they had been back in Christendom for only a few days before they were robbed.

Marco makes no mention in his book about their misfortune; information about it can only be pieced together from other

Polo family documents. But despite generally good relations with traders from all over the Mediterranean world, the rulers of Trebizond had no love of Venetians, and certainly not of Venetians flashing credentials like those of the Polos. The local ruler John II Comnenus had been forced to take to the throne after his elder brother had been kidnapped and held hostage by Abaqa, the father of both Arghun and Kaikhatu, under whose protection the Polos

may have boldly stated that they travelled. Although nominally vassals of the Mongols, the people of Trebizond had no interest in making life easy for Venetians, whose interference a century earlier had caused their exile in the first place. Consequently, either through bogus tolls, trade taxes or outright extortion, the Polos were relieved in Trebizond of goods valued at some 2,000 Venetian gold ducats, before being allowed to go on their way.[151]

Their company was reduced considerably in numbers. Most accounts of the Polos' final journey by sea, from Trebizond to Constantinople, and thence to Negroponte and finally Venice itself, imply that

The Empire of Trebizond

As the Venetians and their Crusader allies were carving up the old Byzantine Empire in 1204, the Byzantine prince Alexius I Comnenus fled to the Black Sea coast, where he called on the military resources of his aunt, Queen Tamar of Georgia. He set up the small empire of Trebizond, centred on the ancient city of Trapezus (modern Trabzon), whose rulers initially claimed to be the rightful heirs to the Byzantine empire. This claim was dropped after the 1280s, but descendants of Alexius would dub themselves the 'Emperor and Autocrat of the Entire East, of the Iberians and of the Transmarine Provinces' until the empire's eventual collapse in 1461.

only the three Polos were left. However, they were probably accompanied by at least one servant, the Petrus Suliman who would be mentioned many years later in Marco's will. They reached Venice in 1295, stumbling onto the quayside after one final sea journey, dressed in outlandish clothes the like of which had rarely been seen in their home town before – knee-high leather boots and silk robes, fastened Mongol-style with round brass buttons, lined with fur and padded against a Siberian winter. They had been away from home for so long, and spent so many years speaking a language other than their own, that they had 'a certain indescribable smack of the Tartar, both in air and accent, having indeed all but forgotten their Venetian tongue'.[152]

The Polos had come home.

The Million Lies

Marco lived for another three decades, but there is significantly less material on the rest of his life than on the period of his famous travels. Not even the story of his arrival back in Venice is his own, belonging instead to Giambattista Ramusio, the compiler of a later Italian version of the book, some 200 years after Marco's death. Perhaps drawing on sources now lost, perhaps simply making it up, it is Ramusio we have to thank for the story of the three men clad in Tartar clothes, stepping gingerly onto dry land back in Venice, and finally returning to the place of their birth. It is Ramusio, too, who tells the next tall tale of Marco's life: that relatives of the Polos initially refused to believe that these three strange, scruffy men were the same trio who had left Venice some 24 years earlier. Doubting cousins, says Ramusio, were soon reassured when the Polos revealed that they were not mere tramps, but men of means. According to one much later folktale, Maffeo's disapproving wife gave one of his scruffy Mongol robes to a local beggar, unaware that he had yet to tell her everything about his travels. But she was soon rushing off to the Rialto to steal back the beggar's clothes, after discovering that the travellers' garments had been deliberately intended not to attract attention. The Polo men ripped the linings of their padded clothes to reveal the many jewels that they had smuggled all the way home from China.[153]

Many? Probably not. Perhaps the Polos did sneak a few valuable items past their inquisitors in Trebizond, but not enough for

A war galley of the type Marco Polo was captured from at the battle of Korčula in 1298.

them to enjoy supreme wealth for the rest of their days. On their return to Venice, they returned to their old profession, trading with middlemen in the east. Ramusio claimed that Niccolo not only remarried, but also had several affairs, and that Marco found himself with three infant half-brothers as he entered his forties.[154]

Marco's name turns up in the records of Venice's merchant fraternity, buying and selling spices and, presumably, other goods. He did not, however, always keep the right sort of company; a 'Marcus Paulo Milion' is mentioned in one 1305 document as the man who posts bail for the suspected (and later convicted) wine-smuggler Bonocio Mestre.

Such friends in low places may have contributed to the most crucial part of Marco's life post-China – his incarceration. Reading between the lines, Ramusio claimed that Marco was probably seized at the battle of Korčula in 1298, but it is equally possible that he was abducted during a far pettier trading skirmish with Genoese rivals. Whatever the true nature of his capture, he was held in Genoa until such time as a ransom could be obtained. Nor was his captivity likely to have been a stereotypical, rat-infested cell; instead, Marco probably lived in relative comfort, able to write home that he was being well-treated and, if Ramusio's later speculations have an ounce of truth, perhaps even to request care-packages including his notes and research materials from home, in order to while away his imprisonment by compiling the book he had long thought of writing.

Marco's fellow prisoner was a native of Pisa, presumed captured in 1294 at the battle of Meloria. Rustichello (also Rusticello or Rusticiana) was a sometime mercenary and poet who had already completed *Meliadus*, a prequel of sorts to the story of King Arthur, which he had based on a book given to him many years earlier by Prince Edward, when the future English king was passing through Italy on his way to the Eighth Crusade. Rustichello appeared to have had some experience of the Holy Land himself, and penned the *Roman de Roi Artus* (*Romance of King Arthur*), extant fragments of which concentrate on the tale of Palamedes, an obscure knight of the Round Table, supposedly of Middle Eastern origin.

Battle of Korčula

As the cities of Venice, Genoa and Pisa continued to jockey for position in the lucrative trade with the east, they fought several battles. Early September 1298 saw a skirmish of the coast of the Adriatic island then known as Curzola, in which a Venetian fleet commanded by Andrea Dandolo was soundly defeated by Genoese vessels under Lamba Doria.

We do not know whose idea it was, but Rustichello seems to have been keen to follow his previous work with a *Romance of the Great Khan* or something similar, and agreed to work with Marco on his book. Their method of working is unclear, but Rustichello appears to have sometimes taken dictation, sometimes summarised Marco's comments, and on other occasions worked from Marco's notes or even forged on ahead without Marco being present at all.

Sometimes, Rustichello's contributions stick out a mile. It is undoubtedly Rustichello the entertainer who is responsible for the tantalising appeals to an imaginary crowd in Marco's book, where an unnamed narrator addresses the reader directly – 'And what should I say? / How can we explain this? / What else do we expect?' Such second-person confrontations seem strange on the page, but are the mark of an accomplished warm-up man, grabbing a crowd's attention and ensuring they are paying attention. So, too, is the opening address of the book, a grandstanding oratory set-up: *Great princes, Emperors, and Kings, Dukes and Marquises, Counts, Knights and Burgesses, and people of all degrees who desire to get knowledge of the various races of mankind and of the diversities of the sundry regions of the world, take this book and cause it to be read to you. For you shall find therein all kinds of wonderful things ... according to the description of Messer Marco Polo, a wise and noble citizen of Venice, as he saw them with his own eyes.*[155]

Compare this opening gambit with that used by Rustichello in his *Meliadus*, and it is plain to see that the passages share the same author: 'Lords, emperors and kings, dukes and counts, and barons and knights and *vavassours* and townsfolk and all the worthy men of this world who are accustomed to taking pleasure in romances, if you take this book and have it read end to end, you will hear all the great adventures which befell the knight errants of the time of Uther Pendragon ... .'[156]

Despite, or perhaps even because of Rustichello's romantic embellishments, Marco's book was to make him famous when

The Saracen Knights

Supposedly a son of King Esclabor of Babylon, the knight Sir Palamedes first appeared in the *Prose Tristan*, a 13th century retelling of Arthurian legend that injected a few elements of Middle Eastern exoticism for the entertainment of audiences with some experience of the Crusades. His brothers Segwarides and Safir also appear in some Arthurian tales. Palamedes himself supposedly converted to Christianity during the quest for the Holy Grail, and became a supporter of Sir Lancelot during Arthur's later years.

Marco Polo dictating his account of his travels to Rustichello while imprisoned in Genoa.

his brief imprisonment was over. The two collaborators parted company on their release, and it seems each went away from their incarceration with a slightly different version of the manuscript. Rustichello's, written in Franco-Italian, seems to have been copied many times at the order of curious patrons, becoming something of a fad among the European upper classes, and drifting into Tuscan, German, Latin and French editions at the hands of unknown translators. In 1312, a Burgundian countess is reported to have paid for the copying, decoration and binding of something called *The Romance of the Great Khan* – possibly a completely different book, but possibly Rustichello's. To this day, some 150 medieval manu-scripts of the book survive.

Marco kept his own version of his book as a mostly private affair, leading to his fame in Venice to develop two contradictory natures. Some Venetians praised him as an educated and observant author, others, perhaps disbelieving the more fantastic elements of the more widely circulated version, began to refer the book dispar-agingly as 'The Million Lies', and its author, Marco Million.

The nickname seems to have originated some time before Marco wrote the book, first turning up in the late 1290s, when uncle Maffeo, perhaps spending some of his smuggled gemstone hoard, bought an impressively palatial residence with its own tower and courtyard. The house was called Il Milione, although the name was thought to be corrupted from Vilioni, the name of a prominent trading family in the town, who may have sold it to the Polos. Somehow, the name was applied to Maffeo's family, and when his nephew Marco began to acquire a reputation as a teller of tall tales, the name stuck.

Marco enjoyed his brief celebrity, but stuck to trading. In 1300, the year of his father's death, he married a local girl, Donata, who eventually bore him three daughters. He traded spices with other Venetians, and became involved in a protracted squabble with uncle Maffeo over the ownership of one of the surviving gold Mongol 'passports'. Eventually, a generation after his return from the east, Marco died in his native Venice, leaving one last document – his will.

Marco bequeathed the bulk of his possessions to his wife and three daughters, Fantina, Bellela and Moreta – much to the annoyance of his cousins, who appear to have expected a little piece of the estate for themselves. His possessions still included numerous souvenirs of his travels, including Tartar bedding, rolls of cloth and brocade, the rosary of a Buddhist monk, the afore-mentioned belt of a 'Tartar knight', and one of the golden Mongol

The Corte de Milion in Venice, the square where Marco Polo lived until his death in 1324.

'passport' tablets. There was even a packet of rhubarb, a plant native to the Gansu corridor in west China, and prized in medieval Venice as a cure for constipation.

Strangest of all, Marco had also kept a Mongol woman's headdress, fitted with gold and studded with pearls. Some have suggested that it was a keepsake from the grateful Princess

Kokachin, given to Marco as a parting gift after reaching her new home in Tabriz. Others have suggested that the headdress was a memento of someone even closer, that Marco's return to Christian Europe left him forever unable to mention.

Considering Marco's repeated notes on women of Asia, and Khubilai Khan's habit of rewarding his loyal servants with wives, is it possible that Marco left a wife behind in the east? He does not mention a Mrs Polo in his book, but nor might he be expected to, as a Chinese or Mongol wife would be frowned upon by Christian Europe, and her mere presence would have invalidated his later marriage to Donata in 1300. *So it comes about that*, writes Marco, after describing the women of China with great nostalgia, *when men return home, they say they have been in {Hangzhou}, that is to say the city of Heaven, and can scarcely wait for the time when they may go back there.*[157]

Marco's will also provided for the freedom of a character who had presumably been his companion for many years, despite never being mentioned in the book. *Peter my slave of the tribe of the Tartars* was freed along with his wife on the death of his master, and given a small sum from the estate, presumably in recognition of years of faithful service.[158] This 'Peter' is a curious figure in the Marco Polo story; some years later, in his own will, he would describe himself as 'Petrus Suliman', implying that he was of Muslim origin, perhaps less a 'Tartar' than a Uighur from Central Asia. Whoever he may have been, if he had been Marco's companion for such a long period, the possibility remains that some of the observations in the book accredited to 'Marco' may have instead come from Peter.

In the decades and then centuries that followed, Marco's reputation often became founded upon misconceptions about his text. Some medieval illustrators of his book paid little heed to the words they were supposed to be illuminating, adding images of strange beasts and races that Marco never mentioned in his original. Others, through illiteracy or inattention to detail, misread portions of his text and illustrated things that weren't there – several editions mistook references to the Polo 'brothers' as descriptions of travelling monks, and depicted them dressed in friars' robes.

In the culinary world, Marco has been credited with numerous 'discoveries' that would have surprised him. He is still often hailed as the man who brought spaghetti and ravioli to China, even though both noodles and stuffed dumplings were both already known in Italy at the time, and had been since an invading Arab army had introduced durum wheat to Sicily in the 9th century. Several Italian words for types of pasta derive directly from Arabic, and it is more likely that both types of food spread east *and* west from Persia or central Asia, and did not originate in China at all.

Nor, contrary to popular belief, does Marco have anything to say in his book about ice cream. The Chinese had been able to cool and freeze foodstuffs since the Tang dynasty, almost a thousand years before Italians started tucking into their *gelati*, but neither fact has anything to do with Marco Polo.[159]

Marco's fame fluctuated towards the end of the 14th century, with his book falling out of fashion, and seemingly left unread to gather dust in a few private libraries. The Mongol Yuan dynasty officially lasted until the 17th century, but only in Mongolia – Khubilai's descendants had been decisively chased out of China by the 1360s. The contraction of the Mongol empire and the re-establishment of Chinese rule in China effectively ended the days when a single authority controlled the entire length of the Silk Road. Travel through the Muslim lands of central Asia became more difficult, rendering Marco's tales of China more likely to be regarded as fiction than fact.

He found new readers at the edges of Europe in the late 15th and early 16th century, when the Portuguese and Spanish finally drove out the Muslims who had occupied Andalusia for so many centuries. With the Iberian peninsula united, at least officially,

A detail of a portrait of Marco Polo painted by Titian (1485–1576).

as part of Christendom, its rulers looked out to the western sea, and wondered if it might somehow be used to take them to the riches of the East. The Portuguese prince Henry the Navigator, the sponsor of many famous voyages in search of a route to the Indies, supposedly received a copy of Marco's book from his brother, who had in turn obtained one from the Venetian senate. Another copy supposedly resided in the library of the King of Aragon, where it became a popular reading choice with Christopher Columbus, and inspired him to seek out the Cipangu of which Marco had written. That, at least is the official story, albeit one which was written sometime later, and with the ulterior motive of explaining why Columbus' mission was not approved many years earlier. The story of a young Columbus poring over Marco's book may have been intended by the 16th-century Spanish to explain later errors – implying that Columbus did not find Japan because Marco's book was *unreliable*, and neglected, in its description of the world, to mention the entirety of the Americas.[160]

Nor did Columbus necessarily read Marco before he made his historic voyage of 1492. A heavily annotated copy of Marco's book is still extant among the collection of Columbus's personal papers in Seville's Biblioteca Colombina, but the writing on it is by several different hands, only one of which may be that of Columbus himself. Columbus' own correspondence implies that he only developed an interest in Marco Polo *after* his first voyage, and that he rifled through every book about Asia that he could find, in search of clues. In particular, he seems to have hoped to find Quanzhou (Marco's Zaiton); in later journeys, he headed further south in the Caribbean, in the expectation that he would reach the Straits of Malacca, and thence Marco's India.

In a modern world, aware not only of America, but of the vastness of the Pacific Ocean, and with more detailed reportage from China and India, Marco's book lost a great deal of its power. Our increasing knowledge of the world also improved our ability to list those things that Marco had got wrong, at the expense of the many things he got right. It was even suggested in some circles that the entire thing was a fake of sorts, and that 'Marco Million' had really idled away the years in a trading post somewhere near between the coast of the Caspian Sea and what is now Uzbekistan, gleaning stories from Persian books and drunken tavern conversations. The beginning of the 21st century finds new scholarship in support of Marco, pointing out that many more recent appraisals of 'errors' in his text have failed to appreciate the languages in which he was working during his stay in China. Marco was not a speaker of Chinese, but of Persian, Turkish and, perhaps, Mongol, and it is through those filters that his comments on the East have reached us.

Today he remains a famous traveller, one of the world's first tourists, and a popular symbol of contact between east and west. His adventures in modern media have included a legendary meeting with Doctor Who and an unlikely team-up with four martial artists in a kung-fu film. His book is still cherished today, despite generations of detractors and disbelievers, and critics who are only able to focus on the things they wish he had mentioned, rather than the things that he actually did. Marco experienced some element of this cynicism in his own lifetime, and indeed was famously urged upon his deathbed to admit that he had falsified parts of his book. It was believed, it seems, by his friends and certain clerics of the Polo family acquaintance, that if Marco died without admitting his deceptions, his soul would be in danger.

Marco's last words showed him defiant, confident and tantalising to the last. *I have not told the half of what I saw.*[161]

Notes

1. The church of Akyndios in Constantinople was rededicated as the basilica of Saint Mark, Saint Nicholas and Saint Mary of the Latins. Had the Polo grandparents' third child been a girl, we might presume she would have been called Maria. Instead, Maffeo unobligingly turned out to be a boy.
2. J Larner, *Marco Polo and the Discovery of the World* (Yale University Press, New Haven: 1999) p 33.
3. Quoted in R Latham (ed), *Marco Polo: The Travels* (Penguin Books, Harmondsworth: 1958), p 11, hereafter Latham, *Marco Polo*.
4. Latham, *Marco Polo*, p 34. See also H Yule (ed), *The Book of Ser Marco Polo The Venetian, Concerning the Kingdoms and Marvels of the East* (John Murray, London: 1871) Vol I, p 4, hereafter Yule, *Marco Polo* I, which omits the final line.
5. Yule, *Marco Polo* I, p 10 (Latham, *Marco Polo*, p 35).
6. Latham, *Marco Polo*, pp 37–8, but see Larner, *Marco Polo and the Discovery of the World*, p 35, which notes that Visconti did not arrive in the Holy Land until 1271, and suggests that this incident was a later interpolation by an over-eager Rustichello (Yule, *Marco Polo* I, p 17).
7. Latham, *Marco Polo*, p 46. Marco calls the town Ayas.

8. S Runciman, *A History of the Crusades, vol. III, The Kingdom of Acre and the Later Crusades* (Penguin Books, Harmondsworth: 1954, repr. 2002) p 340.

9. Yule, *Marco Polo* I, p 22 (Latham, *Marco Polo*, p 39).

10. Yule, *Marco Polo* I, p 25 (Latham, *Marco Polo*, p 39).

11. See also Larner, *Marco Polo and the Discovery of the World*, p 187.

12. Yule, *Marco Polo* I, p 73 (Latham, *Marco Polo*, p 58).

13. Latham, *Marco Polo*, p 65 (Yule, *Marco Polo*, p 93). This appears to refer to the historical Qaraunas or Nigudaris, who were Mongol bandits operating out of a base in southern Afghanistan. They were eventually brought under control by a military campaign of Abaqa, father of Arghun. See J Boyle (ed), *The Successors of Genghis Khan*; translations from Rashid al-Din's *Jami` al-Tavarikh*, dealing with the years 1229–94 (Columbia University Press: 1971) p 139.

14. Yule, *Marco Polo* I, p 102 (Latham, *Marco Polo*, p 67).

15. Latham, *Marco Polo*, pp 68–9 (Yule, *Marco Polo* I, p 115).

16. Latham, *Marco Polo*, pp 77–8.

17. Yule, *Marco Polo* I, p 163.

18. Latham, *Marco Polo*, pp 79–80.

19. Yule, *Marco Polo* I, p 175 (Latham, *Marco Polo*, pp 82–3).

20. Latham, *Marco Polo*, p 88 (Yule, *Marco Polo* I, p 189).

21. Yule, *Marco Polo* I, p 181 (Latham, *Marco Polo*, pp 84–5).

22. Latham, *Marco Polo*, p 91 (Yule, *Marco Polo* I, p 198).

23. Latham, *Marco Polo*, p 102 (Yule, *Marco Polo* I, p 185).

24. Latham, *Marco Polo*, p 108 (Yule, *Marco Polo* I, p 264). Marco's claim of a 'sixteen mile' circumference is an exaggeration, although if he meant 16 *li* (a Chinese unit of measurement) he is very close to the true size of the historical hunting grounds. See S Haw, *Marco Polo's*

China: A Venetian in the realm of Khubilai Khan (Routledge, London: 2006) p 69.

25. Yule, *Marco Polo* I, pp 310–11 (Latham, *Marco Polo*, pp 119–20).

26. Yule, *Marco Polo* I, p 26 (Latham, *Marco Polo*, p 40).

27. Yule, *Marco Polo* I, pp 264–5 (Latham, *Marco Polo*, p 109).

28. Yule, *Marco Polo* I, p 318 (Latham, *Marco Polo*, pp 121–2); see also M Rossabi, *Khubilai Khan: His Life and Times* (University of California Press, Berkeley: 1988) p 151.

29. Yule, *Marco Polo* I, p 331 (Latham, *Marco Polo*, p 128). For the more prosaic explanation concerning the water supply, see Haw, *Marco Polo's China*, p 70.

30. Yule, *Marco Polo* I, pp 331–2 (Latham, *Marco Polo*, p 128).

31. F Wood, *Did Marco Polo Go To China?* (Secker and Warburg, London: 1995) pp 104–5.

32. Yule, *Marco Polo* I, p 367 (Latham, *Marco Polo*, pp 129–30).

33. Marco's text places the account of Ahmad soon after his first arrival in Khanbalikh. However, the chronicles of the Yuan dynasty report the events as occurring in 1282, some years later. Events therefore appear to have unfolded while Marco was away for a *second* summer in Shang-du, with their denouement a few weeks later after he returned to Khanbalikh again.

34. Yule, *Marco Polo* I, pp 370–1 (Latham, *Marco Polo*, p 131). I have followed the suggestion of Haw, *Marco Polo's China*, pp 160–1, in placing Ahmad's murder before Marco's arrival, and the trial afterwards, in order to explain the varying degrees of comprehension and exactitude demonstrated by Marco in his account. A man called 'Polo' (Boluo) testified against Ahmad as part of the investigation, leading some (e.g. Yule, *Marco Polo*, p 377) to assume that Marco had been directly involved. However, this Boluo was no relation.

35. Yule, *Marco Polo* I, p 372 (Latham, *Marco Polo*, p 133).

36. Marco's grasp of facts seems vague here – the names he gives are actually mistranslations of a couple of *ranks*, while the triple-whammy idea of a 'mother, daughter and wife' ravished by the conqueror seems suspiciously close to Chinese poetic licence.

37. Yule, *Marco Polo* I, p 374 (Latham, *Marco Polo*, pp 134–5). See also Rossabi, *Khubilai Khan*, p 201, which notes that anti-Muslim feeling in Khubilai's court persisted until 1287, and led to a dramatic fall in the number of Muslim merchants in China.

38. Boyle, *The Successors of Genghis Khan*, pp 292–3.

39. Boyle, *The Successors of Genghis Khan*, p 294. The chief persecutor of the Muslims was Jesus the Christian (Isa Tarsa Kelemechi, or to the Chinese, Aixie), an Arabic-speaking interpreter who worked for the Mongol administration for his life, and would later form part of a Mongol embassy to Rome.

40. Boyle, *The Successors of Genghis Khan*, p 295. Curiously, even Rashid al-Din may have muddled the chain of events slightly, since even though his account supposedly takes place after the death of Ahmad, 'Ahmad the vizier' is one of the Muslims who pleads for the life of the imam. Note also that citing Koran 2:173 might have allowed the Muslims in China to eat forbidden meat under Khubilai's law, since 'if one is forced by necessity, without wilful disobedience, nor transgressing due limits, then he is guiltless'.

41. Yule, *Marco Polo* I, p 310 (Latham, *Marco Polo*, p 119). Confusingly, Marco places this account *after* his description of the defeat of Nayan (1287), even though it supposedly refers to earlier events.

42. Latham, *Marco Polo*, p 213 (H Yule (ed), *Marco Polo: The Travels* (Penguin Books, Harmondsworth: 1958) Vol II, p 108, hereafter Yule, *Marco Polo* II). Marco's understanding of the fall of Hangzhou was learned long after the fact, when he was shown around many of the sites by a local. Information in this chapter is hence moved from much later in his account and chronology. For Chinese sources on the same events, see Rossabi, *Khubilai Khan*, pp 89–91, and Haw, *Marco Polo's China*, pp 153–4.

43. My account is taken from Rossabi, *Khubilai Khan*, p 91, itself drawing on the chronicle of the Yuan dynasty. It was thus known to Khubilai's ministers, but not necessarily the court as a whole.

44. Latham, *Marco Polo*, p 204.

45. See Haw, *Marco Polo's China*, p 94; also Latham, *Marco Polo*, p 187n, which notes that a battle Marco describes as occurring in '1272', hence before his arrival and presumed to be mere hearsay, is confirmed in Chinese sources as taking place in 1277, hence after his arrival and possibly witnessed by Marco himself. For Chinese sources, see Rossabi, *Khubilai Khan*, pp 92–3.

46. Yule, *Marco Polo* II, pp 3–4 (Latham, *Marco Polo*, p 163).

47. Latham, *Marco Polo*, p 164 (Yule, *Marco Polo* II, p 4).

48. For Marco's version of events, see Latham, *Marco Polo*, pp 166–7 (Yule, *Marco Polo* II, p 9). For the historical parallels and clarifications, see Haw, *Marco Polo's China*, pp 96–7.

49. Latham, *Marco Polo*, p 175.

50. Latham, *Marco Polo*, p 177.

51. Yule, *Marco Polo* II, pp 45–6 (Latham, *Marco Polo*, p 178); see also Haw, *Marco Polo's China*, pp 135–6.

52. Latham, *Marco Polo*, p 201.

53. L Olschki, *Marco Polo's Asia: An introduction to his 'Description of the World', called 'Il Milione'* (Cambridge University Press, Berkeley: 1960) p 105.

54. Even today, most students of Chinese are made to adopt a Chinese name, since European names are often unpronounceable to Chinese speakers. I was originally known in Chinese as *Ke Liwen*, a name selected by my teacher, which I eventually changed to *Cun Zheng*, although some documents still identify me by my sometime pen-name, *Wu Ying*. If I were mentioned in Chinese sources under those names, it is unlikely that I would ever be correctly identified without the aid of an accompanying photograph, or this footnote as a key to the code. Indeed, it is far more probable that references to me would be confused as references to three entirely different people.

55. Latham, *Marco Polo*, p 201.

56. Latham, *Marco Polo*, p 130; for canal dating, see Haw, *Marco Polo's China*, pp 78–9.

57. Latham, *Marco Polo*, pp 156. For knowledge of coal elsewhere in contemporary Europe see Latham, *Marco Polo*, p 157n, Wood, *Did Marco Polo Go To China?*, p 67, and Haw, *Marco Polo's China*, p 64.

58. Latham, *Marco Polo*, pp 196–7.

59. Latham, *Marco Polo*, p 197.

60. Latham, *Marco Polo*, p 198.

61. Latham, *Marco Polo*, pp 198–9.

62. Latham, *Marco Polo*, p 198.

63. Latham, *Marco Polo*, p 202.

64. Latham, *Marco Polo*, p 203.

65. *Yuan Shu*, quoted in Haw, *Marco Polo's China*, p 119. Haw suggests that the census figures in the *Yuan Shu* are from 1290, hence dating from rather late in Marco's sojourn,

but I include the details here in accordance with the order of Marco's own narrative.

66. Latham, *Marco Polo*, p 227.
67. Latham, *Marco Polo*, p 213 (Yule, *Marco Polo* II, p 145).
68. Yule, *Marco Polo* II, p 172.
69. Latham, *Marco Polo*, p 227.
70. Latham, *Marco Polo*, p 227 (Yule, *Marco Polo* II, p 152).
71. Latham, *Marco Polo*, p 228.
72. *Meng Liang Lu*, quoted in E Balazs, *Chinese Civilization and Bureacracy: Variations on a Theme* (Yale University Press, New Haven: 1964) p 95.
73. Latham, *Marco Polo*, p 216 (Yule, *Marco Polo* II, p 160).
74. Yule, *Marco Polo* II, p 164.
75. Latham, *Marco Polo*, pp 226–7 (Yule, *Marco Polo* II, pp 164–5).
76. Latham, *Marco Polo*, p 206.
77. Larner, *Marco Polo and the Discovery of the World*, p 119, and p 203, n 40.
78. Yule, *Marco Polo* II, pp 119–20 (Latham, *Marco Polo*, p 207).
79. Larner, *Marco Polo and the Discovery of the World*, p 63. Larner suggests that the entire deception may have been Rustichello's, hoping to build up the part played by Marco in his own narrative in order to impress doubting and xenophobic French readers. See also Rossabi, *Khubilai Khan*, p 83, which identifies 'Isma'il and Ala al-Din, who designed the artillery for the final assault'.
80. Yule, *Marco Polo* I, pp 288–9 (Latham, *Marco Polo*, p 114).
81. Yule, *Marco Polo* I, pp 299–300.
82. Latham, *Marco Polo*, p 116 (Yule, *Marco Polo*, pp 300–1).
83. Yule, *Marco Polo* I, p 302 (Latham, *Marco Polo*, p 117).
84. Latham, *Marco Polo*, p 117n.
85. Yule, *Marco Polo* I, p 307 (Latham, *Marco Polo*, p 118).

86. Yule, *Marco Polo* I, p 307 (Latham, *Marco Polo*, p 118).

87. Yule, *Marco Polo* II, p 393 (Latham, *Marco Polo*, p 317). For the authenticity of the story and comparative sources, see Rossabi, *Khubilai Khan*, p 252.

88. Yule, *Marco Polo* II, p 394 (Latham, *Marco Polo*, p 318).

89. Yule, *Marco Polo* II, p 395 (Latham, *Marco Polo*, p 319).

90. Yule, *Marco Polo* II, pp 199–200 (Latham, *Marco Polo*, p 244).

91. Yule, *Marco Polo* II, p 200 (Latham, *Marco Polo*, p 244).

92. Latham, *Marco Polo*, p 201.

93. Yule, *Marco Polo* II, p 200 (Latham, *Marco Polo*, p 244).

94. Yule, *Marco Polo* II, p 209 (Latham, *Marco Polo*, p 248).

95. Latham, *Marco Polo*, p 247 (Yule, *Marco Polo* II, pp 204–5).

96. Yule, *Marco Polo* II, p 201 (Latham, *Marco Polo*, pp 244–5).

97. Yule, *Marco Polo* II, p 201 (Latham, *Marco Polo*, p 245).

98. Yule, *Marco Polo* II, p 204 (Latham, *Marco Polo*, p 246).

99. Haw, *Marco Polo's China*, p 162.

100. Latham, *Marco Polo*, p 331.

101. Latham, *Marco Polo*, p 42.

102. Yule, *Marco Polo* II, p 68 (Latham, *Marco Polo*, p 185). For the historical background to Narathihapate's resistance, see Rossabi, *Khubilai Khan*, pp 218–19.

103. Yule, *Marco Polo* II, p 67 (Latham, *Marco Polo*, p 186).

104. Yule, *Marco Polo* II, p 228 (Latham, *Marco Polo*, p 254).

105. Latham, *Marco Polo*, p 242.

106. Latham, *Marco Polo*, p 243.

107. Yule, *Marco Polo* II, p 226 (Latham, *Marco Polo*, pp 252–3).

108. Latham, *Marco Polo*, p 237.

109. Latham, *Marco Polo*, p 237.

110. Ibn Battúta, *Travels in Asia and Africa* (Routledge and Kegan Paul, London: 1929 [1984 repr.]) p 187.

111. Latham, *Marco Polo*, p 239.

112. Latham, *Marco Polo*, p 238.

113. Yule, *Marco Polo* I, p 30 (Latham, *Marco Polo*, p 42).

114. Yule, *Marco Polo* I, pp 30–1 (Latham, *Marco Polo*, p 42).

115. Yule, *Marco Polo* I, p 31 (Latham, *Marco Polo*, p 43).

116. Latham, *Marco Polo*, p 45 (Yule, *Marco Polo* I, p 34). Marco's claim to have a Chinese princess with him is not mentioned in any other source, nor is it corroborated by Persian accounts that otherwise confirm the Kokachin story; see Yule, *Marco Polo*, p 36.

117. Yule, *Marco Polo* I, p 313.

118. Yule *Marco Polo* I, p 33 (Latham, *Marco Polo*, p 43).

119. Latham, *Marco Polo*, p 254.

120. Lathan, *Marco Polo*, p 254.

121. Latham, *Marco Polo*, p 245n; see also Rossabi, *Khubilai Khan*, p 219.

122. Latham, *Marco Polo*, p 251.

123. Latham, *Marco Polo*, p 258.

124. Yule, *Marco Polo* II, p 227 (Latham, *Marco Polo*, p 253).

125. Latham, *Marco Polo*, p 259.

126. Latham, *Marco Polo*, p 281. A generation later, ibn Battúta, *Travels in Asia and Africa*, p 259, reports the same things, and notes that a portion of the footprint was vandalised in 'ancient times' by the Chinese, who took the 'big toe' fragment back to Quanzhou. Could this me the same mission Marco described?

127. Latham, *Marco Polo*, p 284.

128. Latham, *Marco Polo*, p 281.

129. Yule, *Marco Polo* II, p 258 (Latham, *Marco Polo*, p 281).

130. Latham, *Marco Polo*, p 284. The 1280s saw a powerful resurgence in Buddhism in the south of China in particular, thanks in part to the behaviour of a Tibetan monk in Khubilai's service, who scandalously plundered old Song dynasty imperial tombs in order to fund a Buddhist revival. See Rossabi, *Khubilai Khan*, pp 196–8.

131. Latham, *Marco Polo*, p 267 (Yule, *Marco Polo* II, p 279).

132. Latham, *Marco Polo*, p 271 (Yule, *Marco Polo* II, pp 281–2).

133. Latham, *Marco Polo*, pp 264–5.

134. Latham, *Marco Polo*, p 267.

135. Latham, *Marco Polo*, p 265.

136. Latham, *Marco Polo*, p 289 (Yule, *Marco Polo* II, p 282). Marco uses the term *domesces* from the same root as our own 'domestic' and 'domicile' – something familiar to his home, and considered more normal than the exotic places he had been.

137. Latham, *Marco Polo*, pp 274–5 (Yule, *Marco Polo* II, p 290).

138. Latham, *Marco Polo*, p 275 (Yule, *Marco Polo* II, pp 290–1)

139. Latham, *Marco Polo*, p 302.

140. Yule, *Marco Polo* II, pp 346–7 (Latham, *Marco Polo*, p 300).

141. Yule, *Marco Polo* II, p 355 (Latham, *Marco Polo*, p 301).

142. Yule, *Marco Polo* II, pp 355–6 (Latham, *Marco Polo*, p 302).

143. Latham, *Marco Polo*, p 327.

144. Latham, *Marco Polo*, pp 69–70.

145. Yule, *Marco Polo* II, p 406 (Latham, *Marco Polo*, p 328). Marco actually lists Kaikhatu's reign erroneously as 'two years' – I have corrected it here.

146. Yule, *Marco Polo* II, p 407.

147. Latham, *Marco Polo*, pp 71–2 (Yule, *Marco Polo* I, pp 134–5).

148. Latham, *Marco Polo*, p 45. Marco seems unaware that Queen Kokachin ruled for less than a year, and died in June 1296 (Yule, *Marco Polo* I, p 36).

149. Latham, *Marco Polo*, p 44. For Rashid al-Din's similarly confusing account of the same events in his *Jami al-Tawarikh*, see Boyle, *The Successors of Genghis Khan*, p 306.

150. Yule, *Marco Polo* I, p 34 (Latham, *Marco Polo*, p 44).

151. Latham, *Marco Polo and the Discovery of the World*, p 43. Our sole source for this is the ongoing dispute it engendered between Marco and his uncle Maffeo, who appears to have

lent him a considerable sum during the impasse, and claimed never to have been paid back in full.

152. H Cordier (ed), *The Travels of Marco-Polo: The Complete Yule-Cordier Edition* (Dover Publications, New York: 1993) vol.1, pp 4–6.

153. Olschki, *Marco Polo's Asia*, p 107n. The husband is not named, but Marco the Elder was dead, Niccolo was a widower and Marco himself had been only 15 when he left Venice, so logically it must have been Maffeo whose wife caused the brief panic, in the unlikely event the story is not fiction.

154. Yule, *Marco Polo* I, p xxxix. Ramusio claimed that Marco's half-brother Matthew had six children, although all appeared to die without issue except the youngest, Maria Trevisano, who inherited all the wealth of the Polo line in 1417. Her great-great grandson, Marc Antonio Trevisano, was chosen as the Doge (ruler) of Venice in 1553. However, Yule, p civ, states that he has 'met with no positive proof that any descendant in the male line … survived Marco himself,' and that instead over-eager writers have muddled Marco's family with a different Polo clan, of no relation.

155. Yule, *Marco Polo* I, p 1 (Latham, *Marco Polo*, p 33).

156. *Meliadus*, quoted in Larner, *Marco Polo and the Discovery of the World*, p 47.

157. Latham, *Marco Polo*, p 216.

158. Wood, *Did Marco Polo Go to China?*, p 128.

159. Wood, *Did Marco Polo Go to China?*, pp 78–9.

160. Larner, *Marco Polo and the Discovery of the World*, p 153.

161. Jacopo d'Acqui, quoted in Larner, *Marco Polo and the Discovery of the World*, p 45.

Year	Age	Life
1254		Marco Polo born, in either Venice or Korčula.
1255	1	William of Rubruck returns from his failed mission to convert the Mongols to Christianity.
1258	4	Led by the Chinese general Guo Kan and the Christian Kitbuqa, Hulagu Khan's Mongol army captures and sacks Baghdad.
1259	5	Niccolo and Maffeo Polo resident in Constantinople's Venetian quarter. Death of the khan Möngke – he is succeeded by Khubilai.
1260	6	Pope Alexander IV issues the Papal bull *Clamat in auribus*. Niccolo and Maffeo Polo relocate their premises to Soldaia in the Crimea.
1261	7	Constantinople recaptured by Michael VIII Paleologus. Venetian quarter razed to the ground. At about this time, Niccolo and Maffeo Polo relocate further east, to Sarai.
1263	9	The Venetian merchant Pietro Vilione draws up a will in Tabriz.
1264	10	Niccolo and Maffeo Polo join an expedition to the Great Khan, Khubilai.
1265	11	Niccolo and Maffeo Polo reach Khubilai Khan's summer residence, probably in Shang-du ('Xanadu').
1267	13	Khubilai recommences military operations against Song China.

Year	History	Culture
1254	The four bronze horses stolen from Constantinople in 1204 are installed in Venice in St Mark's Square. Louis IX returns to France from the Holy Land.	
1255	Henry III of England accepts Sicily for his son Edmund.	Leon Cathedral begun.
1258	Establishment of the English House of Commons (Provisions of Oxford).	Foundation of the Sorbonne in Paris.
1259	Treaty of Paris between Henry II of England and Louis IX of France.	Matthew Paris, *Chronica Majora*.
1260	Muslim Mamelukes defeat the forces of Hulagu Khan at the battle of Ain Jalut near Nazareth.	Cimabue, 'Madonna'.
1261		
1263	Death of Alexander Nevski, Grand Duke of Novgorod.	
1264	Simon de Monfort defeats and captures Henry III of England.	Thomas Aquinas, *Summa contra Gentiles*. Roger Bacon, *De computo naturali*.
1265	Simon de Monfort killed at battle of Evesham.	Birth of Dante Alighieri.
1267		

Year	Age	Life
1268	14	Death of Clement IV.
1269	15	At about this time, Niccolo and Maffeo Polo return to Venice.
1271	17	The Polos leave Venice, taking the teenage Marco with them. Tedaldo Visconti is elected Pope as Gregory X. Pre-empting his actual conquest of China by eight years, Khubilai Khan proclaims the foundation of the Yuan Dynasty.
1272	18	The Polos supposedly pass through Tabriz, planning on taking a ship at Hormuz, before turning back.
1273	19	Mongol siege of the Song base at Xiangyang.
1274	20	First Mongol attempt to invade Japan is thwarted.
1275	21	The Polos reach Shang-du.
1276	22	The Polos reach Khanbalikh (modern Beijing). The Mongol general Bayan captures the infant Song emperor, Gong Di.
1278	24	Song loyalists are forced to flee Fuzhou by ship in the face of a Mongol advance.
1279	25	Realising all is lost at the battle of Yamen, the minister Liu Xufu leaps from a cliff with the child emperor. End of the Song Dynasty.
1280	26	Death of Marco's uncle, 'Marco the Elder'. Aiyaruk, daughter of Khaidu, wins a thousand horses in a wrestling match with a potential suitor.

Year	History	Culture
1268		First recorded reference to eyeglasses, made by Roger Bacon.
1269		
1271	The armies of the Ninth Crusade land at Acre, led by Prince Edward (later Edward I) of England. A young Rustichello is thought to have been among them.	
1272	Prince Edward becomes King Edward I of England.	
1273		Thomas Aquinas, *Summa theologica*.
1274	Guillaume de Beaujeu, Grand Master of the Knights Templar, is ordered to the Council of Lyons to discuss plans for a 'Tenth Crusade'.	Death of Thomas Aquinas.
1275		
1276		
1278	Death of Pope Gregory X ends plans for another crusade.	
1279		Chinese potters develop hard-paste porcelain.
1280		Albertus Magnus, *Summa theologica*.

Year	Age	Life
1281	27	Second Mongol attempt to invade Japan is thwarted. Death of Khubilai's wife, Chabi.
1282	28	The 'Ahmad' Affair in Dadu.
1284	30	Mongol mission to Sri Lanka in search of holy relics of 'Adam' (i.e. Buddha).
1287	33	Rabban bar Sauma and his assistant Marcus, both Chinese-born Turks, visit Europe as ambassadors of the Mongol khan. Nayan rises in revolt against Khubilai Khan
1289	35	Kertanagara, king of Java, insults Khubilai Khan by branding a Mongol ambassador.
1290	36	Census details for the city of Hangzhou are entered in the chronicles of the Yuan dynasty – Marco claims to have been present during the compilation of the data, presumably in the late 1280s.
1291	37	Death of Arghun, ruler of Persia, at Tabriz.
1292	38	The Polos depart from Quanzhou in the company of the Mongol princess Kokachin, intended as a bride for Arghun. A Mongol invasion fleet departs Quanzhou for Java. Marco spends 'five months' in Sumatra.
1293	39	The Mongol invasion fleet commences operations in Java. Taking advantage of thinly spread forced to resist the invasion, Jayakatwang, king of Kediri, attacks and kills Kertanagara, king of Java. Kertanagara's son Vijaya surrenders to the Mongols, but double-crosses them.

Year	History	Culture
1281		
1282	The Sicilian Vespers: massacre of the French in Sicily.	
1284	130 children go missing near the German village of Hamelin, leading to legends about the 'Pied Piper'.	
1287		
1289		Block printing practised at Ravenna.
1290		Dante, *La Vita Nuova*.
1291	Mamelukes capture Acre, ending Christian rule in the East.	
1292		
1293		

Year	Age	Life
1294	40	Death of Khubilai Khan. The Polos reach Persia and travel to Tabriz.
1295	41	Death of Kaikhatu, brother of Arghun. Ghazan, son of Arghun, regains his crown from his uncle Baidu. The Polos are robbed in Trebizond. The Polos reach Venice.
1296	42	Death of Kokachin in Persia.
1298	44	Captured in a battle with Genoa, Marco Polo begins work on his book in collaboration with his fellow prisoner Rustichello of Pisa.
1299	45	Presumed release of Marco and Rustichello.
1300	46	Death of Niccolo Polo. Marco marries Donata Loredana.
1305	51	John of Montecorvino, Archbishop of Khanbalikh, sends a letter back to Rome in the safe-keeping of unidentified Venetian merchants. One 'Marcus Paulo Milion' is named in Venetian documents as an associate of Bonocio of Mestre, a wine-smuggler.
1310	56	Death of Maffeo Polo. His will mentions an ongoing dispute with Marco over a golden tablet.
1311	57	Marco sues his sales agent, Paulo Girardo, over an alleged failure to charge an agreed price on a commission of musk.

Year	History	Culture
1294		Death of Roger Bacon. 'The Mongol Scroll', recording Japanese defeat of Mongol invasions.
1295		Cimabue, 'Madonna with St Francis'.
1296	Edward I defeats Scots at Dunbar: Scottish coronation stone moved from Scone to Westminster.	
1298	Edward I defeats Scots at Falkirk.	
1299	Treaty between Venice and the Turks.	Building of Palazzo Vecchio in Florence begins.
1300	Aztec empire paramount in Mexico. First formula for gunpowder published in the West.	Chang Sun-Feng incorporates elements of several martial arts to create 'kung fu' – a precursor of *tai qi*.
1305		Jean de Mehun, *Le Roman de la Rose*.
1310		
1311		

Year	Age	Life
1312	58	A book called *The Romance of the Grand Khan* is reported in the possession of Mahaut, Countess of Burgundy.
1323	69	A monk in Tibet discovers that he is the former Song child-emperor Gong Di. He publishes a poem about his lost destiny, and is subsequently executed by the Mongols.
1324	70	Death of Marco Polo. His will orders the manumission of Peter, his 'Tartar slave' and companion of 20 years. Most of his possessions are divided among his three daughters, Fantina, Bellela and Moreta.

Year	History	Culture
1312	Treaty of Vienne: Lyons incorporated into France. Pope Clement V orders suppression of the Knights Templar.	
1323		Thomas Aquinas canonised.
1324	First record of cannon being produced in Europe, at Metz.	

Further Reading

For legal reasons, many quotes from Marco Polo's work in this edition are taken from the 1871 Henry Yule translation, which is out of copyright. Since most English-language readers will find it easier to obtain the Latham translation published by Penguin Books, many of my textual references are twofold, including both the version quoted and a place (in parentheses) where another translation might be found.

The Yule version is fine, wonderfully annotated, but with occasional archaisms that I have done my best to excise – I have taken the liberty of dropping words such as *hath*, *ye*, *aught*, and certain capitalised nouns to make his translation more readable to a modern audience. The Latham is better for the general reader, since he makes many artful deletions and conflations to keep Marco's text clear. In some places, I have retained Latham's version because such textual juggling can sometimes lead to a more illuminating passage – in such cases, I give the Yule version in parentheses, instead. For a less abridged version, the reader is directed to the largest versions available, the French edition of the Moule-Pelliot text, and the Yule-Cordier set, which incorporates Henry Yule's translation, as revised by Henri Cordier, along with a set of notes and additions dating from 1920.

There are many books about Marco Polo, but a surprising number are either children's stories or adult travelogues that use his book to justify a road trip through remote regions. Frances

Wood's influential *Did Marco Polo Ever Go to China?* ignited years of speculation and argument, and remains one of the most rewardingly provocative books on the subject. Its central thesis has since, however, been resoundingly dismantled by many authorities, including John Larner in *Marco Polo and the Discovery of the World*. Larner is particularly good on the history of Marco's manuscript, and on the variant editions that suggest Marco and Rustichello not only had different concepts of what their collaboration was for, but kept different versions for their own uses, which have themselves led to some of the supposed 'contradictions' in Marco's account.

Recent work on Marco has drawn on the expansion of scholarship into languages other than Chinese, particularly the Persian *History of the Mongols*, by Rashid al-Din, a man who must surely have met Marco in person, and who would similarly go on to be a writer of great fame; extracts of his work can be found in J A Boyle's *Successors of Genghis Khan*. Stephen Haw's valuable *Marco Polo's China* presents page after page of Persian-Chinese etymology, demonstrating clearly that while Marco may not have known Chinese, he certainly knew China. For a description of Marco Polo's world, Morris Rossabi's *Khubilai Khan: His Life and Times* presents a fascinating description of China under Mongol rule, largely using Mongol and Chinese sources, and offering much confirmation and elucidation of Marco's own writings on the subject.

Primary Sources

Cordier, H (ed), *The Travels of Marco-Polo: The Complete Yule-Cordier Edition*, 2 vols (Dover Publications, New York: 1993).

Hambis, L (ed), *Marco Polo – Le devisement du monde: le livre des merveilles*, 2 vols, texte integral établi par A-C Moule and P Pelliot, version française de L Hambis, introduction et notes de S Yerasimos (Éditions François Maspero, Paris: 1980).

Latham, R (ed), *Marco Polo: The Travels* (Penguin Books, Harmondsworth: 1958).

Yule, H (ed), *The Book of Ser Marco Polo The Venetian, Concerning the Kingdoms and Marvels of the East*, 2 vols (John Murray, London: 1871).

Secondary Sources

Amitai-Preiss, R, and David O Morgan (eds), *The Mongol Empire and Its Legacy* (E J Brill, Leiden: 1999).

Balasz, E, *Chinese Civilization and Bureacracy: Variations on a Theme* (Yale University Press, New Haven: 1964).

Bawden, C, 'Kublai Khan' in *Encyclopaedia Britannica* DVD Edition, 2002.

Beer, J, 'Coleridge, Samuel Taylor' in *Encyclopaedia Britannica* DVD Edition, 2002.

Boyle, J (ed), *The Successors of Genghis Khan*; translations from Rashid al-Din's *Jami` al-Tavarikh*, dealing with the years 1229–94 (Columbia University Press: 1971).

Franke, H, *China Under Mongol Rule* (Variorum Reprints, Aldershot: 1994).

Haw, S, *Marco Polo's China: A Venetian in the realm of Khubilai Khan* (Routledge, London: 2006).

Ibn Battúta, *Travels in Asia and Africa* (Routledge and Kegan Paul, London: 1929 [1984 repr.]).

Kolbas, J, *The Mongols in Iran: Chingiz Khan to Uljaytu 1220–1309* (Routledge, New York: 2005).

Komroff, M, *Contemporaries of Marco Polo: consisting of the travel records to the eastern parts of the world of William of Rubruck (1253–1255), the Journey of John of Pian de Carpini (1245–1247), the journal of Friar Odoric (1318–1330) and the Oriental Travels of Rabi Benjamin of Tudela (1160–1173)* (Jonathan Cape, London: 1928).

Larner, J, *Marco Polo and the Discovery of the World* (Yale University Press, New Haven: 1999).

Maraini, Fosco, 'Marco Polo' in *Encyclopaedia Britannica* DVD Edition, 2002.

Olschki, L, *Marco Polo's Precursors* (Octagon Books, New York: 1943, repr. 1972).

——, *Marco Polo's Asia: An introduction to his 'Description of the World', called 'Il Milione'* (Cambridge University Press, Berkeley: 1960).

——, *Guillaume Boucher: a French Artist at the Court of the Khans* (John Hopkins Press, Baltimore, 1946).

Petrov, M, and Guy Alitto, 'Takla Makan Desert' in *Encyclopaedia Britannica* DVD Edition, 2002.

Prestwich, M, *Edward I* (Yale University Press, New Haven: 1997).

Ross, E, *Marco Polo and His Book* (Proceedings of the British Academy, London: 1935).

Rossabi, M, *Khubilai Khan: His Life and Times* (University of California Press, Berkeley: 1988).

Runciman, S, *A History of the Crusades, volume III, The Kingdom of Acre and the Later Crusades*. (Penguin Books, Harmondsworth: 1954, repr. 2002).

Shiba, Y, 'Sung Foreign Trade: Its Scope and Organization', in M Rossabi (ed), *China Among Equals* (University of California Press, London: 1970).

Wang, M, and Shi Baoxiu, *Tracing Marco Polo's China Route* (China Intercontinental Press, Beijing: 2004).

Wood, F, *Did Marco Polo go to China?* (Secker and Warburg, London: 1995).

Picture Sources

The author and publishers wish to express their thanks to the following sources of illustrative material and/or permission to reproduce it. They will make proper acknowledgments in future editions in the event that any omissions have occurred.

akg-Images: pp 73, 79, 82, 91, 109, 133; Getty Images: pp 32, 37; Mary Evans Picture Library: pp 16; Topham Picturepoint: pp i, iii, 2, 6, 8, 11, 13, 20, 24, 28, 46, 52, 58, 124, 128, 130, 136.

Index

NB All family relations are to Marco Polo unless otherwise stated.

A

Ahmad Fanakati, 42–3, 44, 49, 78

Aiyaruk (daughter of Khaidu), 86–7

Alexander IV, Pope, 9

Arakhan (Mongol general), 95, 96–7

Africa, 118–20

Arghun Khan (great-nephew of Khubilai Khan), 107, 121

Arigböge (brother of Khubilai Khan), 29

Arigh Khaya (Uighur general), 51

Ashikaga Yoshimitsu, Shogun, 94

B

Barka Khan, 9–10, 12, 29

Bayan, General, 48–9, 68

Beaujeu, Guillaume de, Grand Master of the Knights Templar, 18–19

Bérard, Thomas, Grand Master of the Knights Templar, 18

Boucher, Guillaume, 40

Buddha, The, 47, 113–14

Bulagan, Queen, 107

Burma, 99–100

C

Chabi (chief wife of Khubilai Khan), 49, 106

coal, 64

Columbus, Christopher, 136–7

Constantinople, 5–7, 10

D

Duanzong (Song emperor), 51–2

Duzong (Song emperor), 48

MAO
by Jonathan Clements
ISBN 1-904341-09-8 (pb)

The life of the peasant farmer's son who became ruler of the world's most populous nation is one of the most remarkable stories of the 20th century. His leadership of the communist revolution and the establishment of the People's Republic of China in 1949, after two decades of civil war and Japanese invasion, earned him the title of Chairman Mao. Alternately glorified and demonised, not only in the West but also in the China he once ruled, his influence persists to this day.

Jonathan Clements' excellent biography capitalises on new information to tell this remarkable story. He shows how Mao's outdated Confucian education left him resentful of those with modern knowledge and experience of languages and cultures beyond China. How his wilful ignorance of foreign matters and determination to try and defeat any challenge, sowed the seeds of many flawed political decisions and national disasters.

Millions of Chinese people died during the Cultural Revolution 40 years ago, yet he still remains an iconic figure and his influence persists to this day. China is now the single largest market for capitalist products in the world and as Jonathan Clements points out, it is ironic that Mao's picture appears on everything from blankets to Chinese banknotes.